Also by John Frayn Turner

Service Most Silent
VCs of the Royal Navy
Prisoner at Large
Hovering Angels
Periscope Patrol
Invasion '44
VCs of the Air
Battle Stations
Highly Explosive
The Blinding Flash
VCs of the Army
A Girl Called Johnnie
Famous Air Battles
Destination Berchtesgaden
British Aircraft of World War 2
Famous Flights
The Bader Wing
The Yanks Are Coming
Frank Sinatra
The Bader Tapes
Fight for the Sky (with Douglas Bader)
The Good Spy Guide

RUPERT BROOKE

The Splendour and the Pain

John Frayn Turner

Breese Books, London.

First published in Great Britain by
Breese Books (A division of Martin Breese International)
164, Kensington Park Road, London W11 2ER, England

© John Frayn Turner 1992

ISBN: 0 947 533 16 8

Printed and bound in Great Britain by
Biddles Ltd, Guildford and King's Lynn

The following people gave me their personal help during my research for this book and I shall always feel deeply indebted to them: Bertrand Russell, St. John Ervine, Hugh Dalton, Basil Dean, Mrs Lascelles Abercrombie, Mrs Helen Bailey, John Schroder, Headmaster of Rugby School, Librarian of King's College Library, Cambridge University.

I have been given permission to draw on material from the following books. I am most grateful to the publishers concerned:

Collected Poems of Rupert Brooke
(Sidgwick and Jackson)

Letters from America by Rupert Brooke
(Sidgwick and Jackson)

Call Back Yesterday by Hugh Dalton
(Frederick Muller)

Between Two Worlds by John Middleton Murry
(Jonathan Cape)

At Antwerp and the Dardanelles by Henry Foster
(Mills and Boon)

The Golden Echo by David Garnett
(Chatto and Windus)

Looking Back by Norman Douglas
(Chatto and Windus)

For Remembrance by A. St. John Adcock
(Hodder and Stoughton)

Recollections of Rupert Brooke by Maurice Browne
(Alexander Greene)

I have also read the following books with considerable interest: Rupert Brooke: His Life and His Legend by John Lehmann, The Poems of Rupert Brooke by Timothy Rogers, A Little Love and Good Company by Cathleen Nesbitt.

CHAPTER
1

Rupert Brooke was born on the 3rd of August 1887, the year of Queen Victoria's Golden Jubilee. From his adolescence, though, he was vehemently anti-Victorian and detested the brand of imperialism bred by the nineteenth century - his whole being belonged to the twentieth century.

Brooke's birthplace was 5 Hillmorton Road within sight of Rugby School, where his father had started teaching several years earlier. Their home stood only one road away from the School House, which Rupert came to know so well.

His father, William Parker Brooke, the son of a canon, was a man of cleanly conventional vision, although he was known to compose jocund verses in his rare lighter moments. Rupert's mother, Mary Ruth Cotterill, possessed a certain amount of money, over which she exercised the control of a straight and stern mind.

In this formal family of the respectable late-Victorian middle class Rupert came to consciousness. But Hillmorton Road never imprinted more than an early memory, for in 1892, when Rupert was five, Mr Brooke received promotion to housemaster of School Field in Barby Road. So the family moved the few hundred yards and settled into their new home that came with the promotion. Rupert's elder brother, Dick, was eleven by then, and Mrs Brooke had produced a third son, Alfred, when Rupert was three.

Almost as soon as they were installed at School Field, Rupert Brooke revealed his unconventionality by wandering away from the immediate world of the school and exploring everything within walking range. Once he was retrieved down by the Avon, another time roaming in the fields surrounding Rugby with his old bull terrier, mysteriously named Mister Pudsey Dawson.

As soon as Rupert was old enough he was sent away to

Hillbrow preparatory school. Just before he joined, Mrs Brooke led him into Rugby town to be photographed with his large, stiff Eton collar protruding over a velvet jacket. Completing the boy's correct attire were knickerbockers and long stockings. Rupert, aged seven, stood with his hands on his hips, his hair combed straight towards the front without a parting. He did not like that garb; in particular, he hated his Eton collar with its stiff, restricting feel, but as yet he was too young to rebel openly against such senseless conventions.

By 1898, he had graduated to a dark coat and waistcoat, with lighter trousers. He wore a large tie over the inevitable stiff collar. Each year he resented those collars more. Now, at eleven, his proud, perfect features were well formed, and his lips might sometimes be parted with the upper one sloping slightly towards the centre.

Sir Gilbert Scott, the architect of School Field, recalls him at this time as delightful and intelligent. To these rare qualities for a boy could be added independence. For in 1899 he supported a local meeting in favour of the Boers! His mother told him off for trying to bully his younger brother into similar support, but Rupert countered with agility that it was she who was bullying for attempting to inflict her views on him.

Rupert was becoming an acute observer of life with an enquiring intellect. Already he had developed a love of freedom and the unconventional which could be ascribed at least in part to a revolt against the respectability of his background. He could not be bothered with the religious pieties of the family and now his hate of formal clothes exploded into a fetish for an open necked shirt wherever possible, and running about barefooted in summer. Rupert had a mind of his own: sensitive and strong.

Trim took the place of Mister Pudsey Dawson; the century closed; and Rupert moved on from Hillbrow to Rugby itself. Back home to his father's house and under the parental eyes. His natural and growing enthusiasm and élan overcame any real resentment at the restrictions of Rugby and all the while he gradually grew more conscious of his surroundings, his attitude towards them, his feelings for them: aware, if not yet articulate or able to express those feelings.

Rupert looked up at the tall three-storey house as he returned to it in July 1901 for the summer holidays. This would be home over the next five years, home and school interwoven through his adolescence. School Field, set in a corner of the peaceful playing fields, with its trio of dormer windows on the top floor almost cloaked in ivy. It was all impressive, enduring, permanent, secure: the perfect place to grow up, to remember with joy.

Although almost palatial from the outside, it lacked many amenities, having cold stone passages on the ground floor and a generally dark air about it. In spite of this Rupert loved every crevice and seemed to be glad of its safety. He loved the part formal, part wild garden especially. The whole situation, looking on to the playing fields called Big Side, was ideal. Over on the left there rose the sharp strange outlines of a monkey-puzzle tree; beneath it, the fragrance of flowers at their late-July zenith; but best of all he liked the long grass path that he made his own by constant use. He would wander up and down its length, reading as he went. Old pergolas threaded overhead. Round to the right of School Field he could see the Island - the large grass mound supporting the famous clump of trees that gave summer shade to the spectators at school games. For Rugby thrived on cricket and also gave its name to the brand of football played with the hands as well as the feet. The game actually arose out of an incident in the autumn of 1823, on these very grounds, when one William Webb Ellis, while playing in the Close, caught the ball, but instead of retiring back and kicking it according to the rules of those times, had the extreme temerity to run with it clasped in his arms towards the opposing goal!

Rupert's fourteenth birthday passed and so did that summer when he was suspended between his preparatory school days and the Rugby years starting in September. He relished every high-summer day and realised that here was a turning-point in his life. The next would come exactly five years later as he left Rugby, but for the moment he stood on its threshold. Not only the threshold of Rugby, but the whole Edwardian decade which coincided with the start of the Michaelmas term.

While still at Hillbrow, Rupert had scribbled secretive

9

verses; now with Rugby as stimulus and setting, he turned more toward this world. At the same time, he had to accustom himself to the teeming, lunging life of six hundred boys. In the process, he began to lose a lot of the introversion apparent when younger. He lived a normal school existence but, as always, he never became swamped by tradition or convention for their own sake. He might be impressed at the sense of solidity around him in the shape of big buildings; but he also ridiculed the incongruous castellations and giant Gothic excrescences of much of the monumental architecture. The rest accepted it, or more likely, never noticed it: Rupert questioned and commented.

For the first year or two, few of the boys in School Field realised that anyone out of the ordinary was among them. Rupert was still inclined to be quiet much of the time, though he could mix well and proved himself good at games.

Although he lived much as anyone else, gradually those around him became aware of little differences about him. Instead of joining a group going 'down town', he often went only as far as the newly-opened Temple Library. He would vanish eagerly into the lofty single-storey structure to read the reviews of the latest books. Here he sat content, occasionally glancing up to the high, arched windows and beyond to the trees on the Island. Books, and poetry in particular, were already in his essence.

H.F. Russell-Smith, one of the boys in the same house then, remembers him reading Walter Pater and other authors quite foreign to his companions. When he was not in the library, where even the tick of the clock in the corner echoed around the room, Rupert walked to and fro along his grass path, reciting the metre of a poem to the pounding of his step. Early in the century he discovered Oscar Wilde, Ernest Dowson and Swinburne. Rupert rhapsodised over Swinburne to his house friends, who on the whole adopted an adamant indifference.

'The trouble is that you're all a lot of Philistines' he complained cheerfully.

He grew his hair longer than was usual and he won a school scholarship. However books did not exclude games. In 1903 he played cricket for the House XI at an age younger than anyone else in the team and later helped School Field to become Cock House in both football and cricket.

As Rugby and Rupert came to terms, he began to develop an extraordinary vitality which showed itself in a boundless enthusiasm and boisterous sense of fun. When he wrote to his friends this sense of the absurd was revealed in burlesques of masters or boys, or parodies of himself.

Rupert usually seemed to be hurrying somewhere, when he was not studying. He and Russell-Smith used to dash across from School Field so as not to be late for chapel. Then after the day's work, another rush to Big Side prayers, when Rupert would sing the evening hymn at the top of his voice with a glorious disregard for tune.

One day when a sheep became entangled in one of the cricket nets, Rupert rushed on the Close to release the creature which was calling pitifully for help. Generally the boys saw him with a book, for while they were going for a walk or a bathe, he would be reading.

Rupert got through a great deal but neither Rugby nor Cambridge persuaded him to pursue a steady scholastic course. He preferred to study what interested him most - seldom the conventional classics or the syllabus set! A little later he wrote several chapters of an enormous Romance while he should have been busy with school work. The Rugby scene was helping him to develop; but the things to spark his senses were the white moonlight strangely reflected on the glass roof of the observatory, or the huge elm beside the chapel, rather than the Greek epics.

By the time he was sixteen, Rupert was writing fluent adolescent verse and in the spring of 1904 came his earliest recorded work, 'The Pyramids'. This he composed for the annual prize poem for the school and though it did not win, he received an additional award, as it was considered so nearly equal to the winning entry.

Imperfect and immature as it was, the poem promised much for the future, with lines like:

And heard the roll and clangour of the years
bearing on men and their little hopes and fears.

And later:

> Proud in the girdle of her Seven Hills,
> Indomitable Rome.

Perhaps the most promising mark was that he tried to avoid the cliché and the merely pretty phrase. In his original manuscript, one line read:

> child of the newborn France, the Corsican.

When his mother had the poem privately printed in May 1904, he decided to change 'newborn' to 'newgrown'. Mrs Brooke, although she never for a moment understood her son properly, apparently recognised that he had some talent by arranging for the poem to be circulated to their friends.

Three of his five years at Rugby had fled in the flurry of daily school routine. In the Michaelmas term, he saw himself in print for the first time more or less publicly. A touring company performed 'As You Like It' in the Town Hall early in the term and Rupert contributed an unsigned notice of the play to the school magazine 'The Meteor' on November 1. Throughout the ten years left of his life, Rupert maintained a growing interest in the poetic theatre, most of all, the Elizabethan poet-playwrights.

The earliest examples of Rupert's poetry were published in a second school publication 'The Phoenix' which survived for only three issues between 1904 and 1905. A prose offering entitled 'A child's guide to Rugby School' showed he was no respecter of persons or place but whether this could have been connected with the early demise of 'The Phoenix' is not known! One of its successors, 'The Vulture', however, was definitely forbidden by the school authorities.

He initialled his more serious poems that winter 'E.R.T.' - the last three letters of his Christian name - and one of these 'The Return' appeared in the next number of 'The Phoenix'. This is the poem beginning:

> Long had I dwelt in dreams and loneliness.

The others identified by the initials at this era were 'Afterwards' and 'In the End', the latter remaining unpublished.

These early poems, scribbled in pencil in exercise books, convinced the strong-minded and puritanical Mrs Brooke that Rupert would benefit from travel. So during the Christmas holidays and the early part of the spring term, 1905, he spent some weeks in Italy and France, the first of numerous Continental excursions he was to make over the next six or seven years.

Rupert was reaching an educated adolescence and was about to embark on a phase of slight disillusion with the world. Real or assumed, this continued on and off for about two years but was only a passing pose of youth. Anyway, he deigned to admire Botticelli, though expressing regret that the painter was in fashion with most people just then.

On this Italian trip, he was one of a party of thirty young Britons, mostly girls, and he actually enjoyed himself more than he admitted to his family. His cards home to them were brief in the extreme but to his special school friends, with whom he now felt a closer link, he wrote at length on Italy and the arts. This 'disillusioned' spell was probably no more than a front to cover the transition from boyhood to man while values in general were tending to shift in consequence.

His intellect was awake. Now his emotions became conscious. At Fiesole the party paused to discuss the merits of Browning and then as the sun started to set westward of Florence, they watched the river Arno down in the distance, 'a writhing dragon of molten gold'.

These then were the formative years. He grew in mind and body; developed a natural charm with magnetic manner and features to match; and encouraged an innate sense of humour, which showed itself later in the whimsical undertones to much of his lyric poetry. Now, neither accurate nor studious in the accepted meanings, he preferred parodying a master to filling a notebook with lightly exotic - and erotic - fragments of verse.

By 1905 most traces of his former reticence had gone. He realised that poetry would be his profession and he was discovering a burgeoning ability to express himself.

Rupert still could not quite reconcile Rugby with his views on various things. But instead of rebellion, he favoured subtler means of overcoming the gulf between school and himself. He loved colour - and coloured ties. These were not allowed at school, but he cleverly got around the restriction by wearing large scarves at the neck of open-necked flannel shirts. This question of clothes might have seemed small and silly to some people but to Rupert it became a matter of principle - though not ponderously so. He wanted the freedom to wear what he liked, just as later he felt the need to live as he liked. And in both cases, he managed to solve his dilemmas with a sly smile. It was no good being too serious about serious matters but that did not mean he felt any less deeply about them.

Early in May Rupert completed his second attempt for the prize poem, choosing as his subject 'The Bastille'. When he heard he had won, he scampered down the stone passage of School Field to tell his mother, who was pleased yet still surprised at such an unlikely talent in a son of hers. Such strange ideas he had, too, she mused.

Rupert won volumes of poems by Browning and Rossetti and had to recite the poem on Speech Day, 24 June. Fortified by the proximity of his friend, the musician Denis Browne who sat at the piano for duty later in the proceedings, Rupert read:

Sullen athwart the freedom of the skies

It was clear he had progressed one year nearer to pure poetry. The poem appeared in a publication for private distribution, in the pamphlet of prize compositions recited on that day in New Big School on the midsummer air and also in the last issue of 'The Vulture'.

Rupert's critical faculties were ripening too, for he changed one or two lines in the printed version. Two other small alterations were the correction of the word 'irresistable' to '-ible', and the omission of a comma between the final two words:

and Time Eternity.

Still we grope, he wrote. The poet was still emerging through the more mundane duties of the Cadet Corps and games.

A few days after school broke up in July Rupert found himself standing stiffly to attention, his legs constricted in the puttees of his Rifle Corps uniform. He tried to ease each leg in turn, and cursed gently at such an uncomfortable uniform. Looking less debonair than usual, his khaki cap covered the mop of golden hair which seemed to be lightening by a tone each successive summer. The Cadet Corps went to the Public Schools' Camp for a strenuous, disciplined course. Rupert did his duty, but with the world in a slumbrous peace, it all seemed rather silly to him.

One of the first things he did the following term was to send a signed copy of 'The Bastille' to St. J.B. Wynne Wilson, who had helped Rupert and quoted its last lines in his farewell sermon of the summer term before leaving Rugby for the headmastership of Haileybury.

He told Wynne Wilson of the passing of 'The Phoenix' and 'The Vulture', adding that 'The Venture' had just appeared. The aims of this were literary, Rupert assured him, but it also included an article on school football so that the illiterates would be tempted into buying it and be educated unawares! The first issue in October published his poem 'The Lost Lilies'.

Rupert started his last school year as a high-spirited intellectual eighteen-year-old, still subject to occasional bouts of reserve or remoteness. During the winter of 1905-06, he played the game which was almost a religion with the boys - rugby football - and gained a place in the First XV with this reference against his name - 'R. C. Brooke (11st 12lbs.), a reliable centre three-quarter who, though not brilliant, is usually in his place, and makes good openings. He tackles too high.'

Many times that winter, Rupert skidded fast towards the opposing goal-line before passing out to his waiting wing three-quarters. He may not have been great at games but the Rugbeians of the mid-Edwardian era remember him as a good man in a tight corner and one who could not stand slackers in a team. Even if he was not wildly keen on rugby Rupert always tried hard.

15

By this time, most of the house had come under his spell. They accepted his interests, particularly since he was invariably so natural and didn't mind them making fun of his poetry. But it was his personal presence and charm that attracted them most; few could resist it.

During this school year he was elected head of the house and everyone under him was affected by his radiant personality. The spirit in School Field that year made the house different from any other and was probably due to the two Brookes - father and son. The situation could easily have been awkward for both of them but, mainly because of Rupert's qualities, it never was for an instant. He remained loyal to his parent while contriving not to make the rest of the house aware of his relationship to their housemaster. The secret lay in his immense sense of fun for he never took any teacher very seriously. And the boys of School Field knew that they could rely on him never misinterpreting their attitude towards Mr Brooke.

Outside the house, Rupert's abilities became known and appreciated by the Upper Bench and a few of the specialised masters. He was in the sixth form now, and developing his debating powers at a series of society motions during the winter.

Five years had flown in a flash of poetic peace, traditional games, and the Rugby routine. Rupert was remembered 'with a ball in his hand and a book in his pocket'. The legend was unfolding.

Just before Easter, 1906, he had an attack of ophthalmia. He and another senior were laid up in School Field as the sanatorium was full. A week went by without improvement to either of them until Mr Brooke charged in as the family doctor was examining them and told him that it was his fault. The two men's tempers rose, as Rupert and the other boy could only lie and listen. After this, they turned the corner and Rupert was packed off to Venice to recuperate for a fortnight. His eyes were better again there and he could see and sense the full magic as he leaned over a bridge and watched his reflection softly stirring in the water below.

Rupert was getting used to these changes of scene, and relied on them to widen his poetic powers.

Then back from Venice to the other Island, at Rugby,

as late daffodils dotted the foot of the trees. Sitting sheltered and secure beneath their branches in the first week of the new term - his last at school - he completed his English historical essay for the King's Medal for Prose. Its title was: 'England's Debt to William III'. In a characteristic afterthought, Rupert wrote 'History repeats itself: Historians repeat one another'. The essay holds no special significance yet it won the medal with some ease.

The previous summer, his hair had only just started sprouting around the tight, white school cricket cap. Now it was longer and parted precisely in the middle, falling freely to either side. He revelled in his open shirts and self-striped sports trousers. Clad like this, he was photographed as one of the First XI, his legs crossed casually with confidence.

The last golden summer slipped away. The team went up to London for the annual match against Marlborough, whom they beat convincingly by 227 runs. It was an idyllic week, with Lords looking its midsummer greenest. Floral dresses were scattered colourfully around the ground while parents and friends strolled over to the Tavern for a drink or snack.

Rugby batted first and scored 291. Rupert went in tenth as he was being played for his bowling. He walked the long route out from the pavilion to the crease and grinned at the Marlborough wicket-keeper who had just made a catch. Five minutes later he was walking back again for a duck! Marlborough replied with 231 and then the Rugby second innings came to a close at a declared score of 240 for 6 wickets. Rupert did not get another chance to bat. Marlborough were 300 runs behind, and in their second innings were routed 73 all out. Rupert held a couple of catches at a vital stage in the match. The second was a hard, stinging chance which he caught with one hand. He had justified Rugby's memory of him as having 'a ball in his hand'. The last wicket fell at a quarter to six as the shadow of the pavilion was moving across the outfield. Suddenly it was all over - and the remaining few weeks of term cascaded from the calendar.

One of Rupert's house friends at School Field has said:

I have always felt in myself that Rupert of all people at school gave me an inkling of what a full life really meant. He, with no appearance of superiority or attempt at preaching - as keen as any of us on all the immensely important events in school life and always ready for a rag - impressed us weaker brethren as no-one else could, with the fact that these things were not all, not even the most important. And the best thing about him was that he was not out to impress us.

Rupert looked with longing at Rugby that July, at all its oddly lovable buildings where Samuel Butler, Matthew Arnold, Clough, Landor and Charles Dodgson (Lewis Carroll) had trod. He looked with sudden significance. It was all over. In 'The Meteor' is his memory of it, as he recalled soon afterwards:

I had been happier at Rugby than I can find words to say. As I looked back at five years I seemed to see almost every hour golden and radiant, and always increasing in beauty as I grew more conscious; and I could not and cannot hope for, or even quite imagine, such happiness elsewhere. And then I found the last days of all this slipping by me, and with them the faces and places and life I loved, and I without power to stay them. I became for the first time conscious of transience and parting, and a great many other things.

This same mood prompted him to write 'The Farewell' later that year, a poem which ends:

> But ... the things we leave behind,
> *They* are the best.

Appropriately his last act before leaving Rugby was to give a lecture devoted to modern poetry on his final Sunday. Neither muddled nor maudlin, this proved to be a lighthearted living hymn of praise for poetry in terms of the world around them: the world of Yeats and Dowson.

Another summer holiday, and then, from the spreadeagled silhouettes of familiar Rugby landmarks, he took a train to Bletchley and changed for Cambridge: a

new skyline and a new life.   He was nineteen, R. C.
Brooke, freshman of King's College, a boy no more.

CHAPTER
2

As Brooke turned into King's Parade with its famous facade of small-paned bookshop windows, and saw the stone College buildings in the pale amber afternoon he suddenly experienced a wave of reticence and regret. He missed his old school friends, dispersed since the summer term ended and he had yet to find fresh ones here. The lawns were beginning to lose their summer colour and even the Backs at first sight seemed barren, the water dank and dark. Leaves curled aimlessly across the grass. Undergraduates filled the pavement, moving and milling with just as little purpose. He shivered slightly as he walked into King's. It was all so strange. Here life had gone on for centuries already. But his own life at King's dated only from today, from this very moment when he walked past the porter's lodge and enquired after his rooms. Brooke felt fragile, alone.

Then he pulled himself together and found the rooms as an autumn mist was beginning to seep upstairs and cloud the gas-lights on the landing. After tea and toast, and with the lamps lit, things looked warmer, cosier again. He unpacked his things and started sorting the little pile of books he had brought with him from Rugby. They did not fill the shelf provided so he spaced them out a bit. Soon the room would be bulging with books, borrowed or bought, and the shelf would be swamped with new-found favourites. This room was his immediate world. What lay beyond was hidden in the dusk, on what lay ahead Brooke did not want to dwell. He fell asleep that first night to the sound of the city's chimes and when he awoke it was to the swelling sounds of a new term in a university college.

Still the strangeness lingered though. Throughout his life he had these occasional spells of deep depression as if compensating for the intense level at which he lived. This one found expression in the 'decadent and disillusioned' pose, as practised at Rugby. He hung pictures by Aubrey

Beardsley around his walls and began to keep eccentric hours to match - not recognising any time before noon! There were a couple of other Rugby freshmen at the University, too, one of them Hugh Russell-Smith. Brooke sought out both these kindred souls and also wrote mock laments to his friend St. John Lucas - another young 'decadent' - and to his cousin in Godalming, Erica Cotterill. All the people at Cambridge were too terribly clever and witty and wearying: this was the gist of his complaint. He lost interest in games without the old loyalties of Rugby and School Field; disliked discipline as heartily as ever; and still found imposed reading became oddly onerous. He alleged that he did not feel able to read or write to any purpose yet in the first month or two at Cambridge he composed four recorded poems, including one early essay in the manner of 'ugliness' of which he was subsequently sometimes accused. 'The Song of the Beasts' was the title and its lines contained this typical couplet:

> Though mad whispers woo you, and hot hands cling,
> And the touch and the smell of bare flesh sting

Already, at nineteen, he was looking back on a girl friend of his Rugby days in another poem of the same season, 'The Beginning'. Many times they had strolled by the banks of the Avon and stopped beside the still stream. This is more lyrical than 'The Beasts' yet it is tinged with the regret he felt for those intimate, carefree years. The autumn mood of melancholy shows sadly in this little lyric:

> And I loved you before you were old and wise,
> When the flame of youth was strong in your eyes,
> - And my heart is sick with memories.

Brooke's introspection wore off as the term wore on. Strangely enough, he exchanged a paternal housemaster for a dean who was an uncle. His Uncle Brookie was Dean of King's so the family authority still lingered over him, if indirectly.

He met fresh fellow-spirits in King's. Not everyone was wearisome after all. On the first Sunday of the term he ran into Hugh Dalton on the steps of the Provost Lodge and the friendship which grew between these two was one of a number developed at Cambridge. Dalton went up to King's the same term as Brooke; he was the same age, just twenty-three days younger; and he loved poetry as passionately. No Cambridge friendship meant more to Dalton than Brooke's over the next four years, and the relationship was reciprocal. Dalton possessed as great a feeling for fun then as half a century later, and was partly instrumental in helping Brooke over his first-term gloom.

Brooke could not enthuse over the syllabus, but nor could he repress for long his old *joie de vivre*, so as an outlet for it he branched into the dramatic field. His interest in poetic drama dated back several years already, and he persuaded the producer to give him a small part in the 'Eumenides' of Aeschylus, played in the original Greek. He hoped to take the role of Hermes, but this went to someone more experienced and he was cast instead as the herald in the final scene.

He was clad in classical dress of striking red, blue and gold, complete with wig, buskins and clarion. His little band of friends sat spellbound in their seats as, at the appointed second, he appeared in the midst of the proceedings and raised the instrument to his lips with a flourish while the note sounded off-stage. He was seen for only a minute or so yet he looked as if he had stepped straight over the centuries from the ancient Hellenes. Arthur Benson, Master of Magdalene College, remembered that he seemed wholly without nerves. Although making a fine statuesque figure, dignified and self-possessed, Brooke monotoned his part in a Grecian chant without flexibility or dramatic sympathy! Perhaps he preferred his mother tongue as his own verse was already proving essentially English. Another less favourable comment came in a review of the play which noted that 'a herald made a pretty figure spoilt by a glassy stare'.

Hardly an auspicious initiation. Brooke's only other venture that season was with the Cambridge Amateur Dramatic Company, playing a minor part in 'She Stoops to Conquer'.

As an additional outlet in revolt against the dreary syllabus, Brooke and Dalton, with other equally staunch spirits, founded an exclusive little set christened the Carbonari, or charcoal burners, after an early nineteenth century revolutionary society in liberty-seeking Italy. Belying its inflammatory name however, the Carbonari held harmless meetings to read papers and poetry and then discuss them. Arthur Waley, later an authority on Oriental poetry, was elected a member in his first year. The dozen members also included Philip Noel-Baker and J. Steuart Wilson.

At one of their earliest meetings, Brooke read some of his poems to them. None had then been published - not even in Cambridge magazines to which he became an energetic contributor - in fact, one or two he read literally as the ink dried. More often they were scribbled in pencil on any scrap of paper about the room. This did not mean they were composed hurriedly, for he was always a careful craftsman. What he would be doing as he jotted down words just before reading to them was merely altering a phrase or filling in a blank word - a favourite finish of his.

This first time the Carbonari heard Rupert recite was something none of them forgot. The group were scattered casually in the shadowy folds of the room, the light focused on Brooke by the little lamp. The light caught the top of an occasional mug of beer and was reflected darkly. A few half-eaten hunks of cheese and slices of bread lay on plates. The evening was late. Outside, the weather cold.

Then he began to read. The combined sense of the poem and Brooke's voice moved Dalton deeply as he listened amazed at their imagery and music. Most of them felt the same. Dalton knew Rupert could create poetry but until this instant in a room of King's College, he had no idea of its full beauty. Brooke with his flowing rhythm, perfect stress, and sense of drama read verse to a small group far better than anyone Dalton had ever heard. When he finished a poem, a moment's quiet prolonged the mood before a murmur of voices applauded the lines just faded from the air. These were the moments in time which Brooke was later able to recapture in whole poems. 'The Vision of the Archangels', 'Day that I have Loved' and 'The Beginning' were the best of this juvenilia, which was immature yet remarkable for its promise. These three were Dalton's own favourites from the period and his roguish features sharpened in anticipation as he heard Brooke begin them on those winter nights. The kind of nights which would stay with them as impressions of the whole meaning of their early Cambridge years, when life was young and they were eager to meet it.

Reciting poetry in a larger gathering Brooke sounded less effective and both Russell-Smith and Dalton beat him at a later date to win the Winchester reading prize. This loss of quality could be compared to his acting ability which was much more vital in the relaxed and intimate circle of a rehearsal than at the actual performance.

Meanwhile, Brooke began to lose his autumn nostalgia for the green playing fields of Rugby, his personal grass path and those architectural absurdities. He and Dalton talked modern poetry much of their spare time. Both came to Cambridge rather drunk with Swinburne. Now they felt it was time to grow up and move on towards the fresh fields of Housman's 'Shropshire Lad', for instance, which they read to each other in their rooms to get the full effect. As Dalton said: 'We went into the Celtic Twilight with the early Yeats and stayed to see Synge's plays acted as the daylight grew.' Then Brooke introduced Dalton to Hilaire Belloc who was later to materialise miraculously before them, larger than life.

Another writer, of a different sort, whom they hero-worshipped was Charles Masterman. They thought of him as the young leader of the Radical-Socialist wing of the Liberal Party. Brooke belonged to no political party or society yet but, ever since that pro-Boer demonstration, he clearly held radical views. Before he left home he had helped the Liberals locally in the 1906 general election, editing an election paper which appeared on alternate days and canvassing all and sundry in respectable Rugby. This was mainly just for the fun of it, however, rather than a reflection of political awareness.

Hugh Dalton joined the Fabian Society as soon as he reached Cambridge but Brooke was still more interested in the arts than politics.

So on and off for the rest of the term, Brooke continued playing the 'modern decadent', languishing with copies of Verlaine and Baudelaire, decking his study with green rugs and curtains to match the mood of his Beardsley sketches. He told his friend St. John Lucas that he wanted to complete his set of books by those three decadents - Wilde, Lucas and Brooke! He added that he had given up writing for the moment as there were only ten beautiful words in the English language and he had used them all. He had already written of love too much.

So the term went on till Christmas came, when he fell ill. A friend, Gertrude Lindsay, came round to School Field several times to draw a portrait of him, otherwise nothing happened, he complained. Idleness and indifference irritated him even more than enforced study of the dead classics. For all he wanted was to read poetry, write poetry and, best of all, to live poetry - as he announced to Dalton on one famous occasion. 'You know, Hugh,' Brooke said, 'At rare moments, I have glimpses of what poetry really means, how it solves all problems of conduct, settles all questions of values.'

It was more in this frame of mind that he returned after the vacation. Then, almost at once, the first real sorrow of his life swept aside all self-absorption. His older brother, Dick, who had always looked frail, suddenly died on 13 January 1907. Brooke received the news in his study the next day and automatically returned to Rugby to try and comfort his mother, ill with the shock of it. After he had done all he could, he retraced the journey he had made only a week earlier to Cambridge.

He wanted to be alone. Completely alone. This did much to shake him out of the immature 'decadence' of the previous term but it seemed a high price to pay. He walked around the town, through the bustling market, explored strange parts away from King's, then found himself along the Backs. Pastel sunlight filtered from the January sky as he leaned over a bridge and looked abstractedly down at the water. Dick was dead. What did it mean? Why had it happened? They were not especially close but they had been brothers. So there was something deep in the blood after all. Strange, he thought, how two people can be apart in space and outlook yet be linked like this by the family tie. Dick, Dick. Brooke thought back to their years at home and tried to visualise his face and what they had done together. All he could see was a composite across the years; Dick as a boy, a youth, a man, and now no more.

He threw a loose stone from the bridge into the water and saw his own image in the water shattered into a rippling circle. He walked back to his study.

Rupert still had no time for the Church, but he could not resist stealing into the great chapel at King's one afternoon - its four fingers of Gothic carved stone pointed high to heaven from each corner.

As he moved inside, the late sun came out and, at the same second, Bach was wafted on to the air from the organ overhead. Filtered sound and sun filled the vast vault of glass, stone and wood. Then a chord throbbed through the building and an elation surged, swept into Brooke's body. The notes ended, yet the strength of their sound still hung in the air.

He looked up at the amazing arcs of stone spanning the roof. Eighty feet above him a fine fretwork of stone had stood there suspended for four and a half centuries, interlaced, splaying from the tall walls. His eyes moved down these walls to the rich red and blue of the windows, their slender elegance emphasised in groups of four. Here was peace, apart from any feeling for religion. Peace - and wonder that here it had stood since 1450.

A dramatic division, the deep brown wood organ, with its gold pipes gleaming and pointing high. And the figures of heralds atop the organ, their trumpets gold, too.

Rupert walked down the aisle, under the huge organ loft, as a shadowy silhouette was lighting the choristers' candles, in pairs and singly, behind their protective glass. He saw the low, late sun fall across clusters of candles around the altar; then the great glass window above it. Red, blue and green glass towering toward the roof. He stood there some time, turned, and walked slowly back and out into the air again. The sun was setting round to the right behind the Backs. Life seemed strange - and wonderful.

Brooke determined to occupy his mind to the limit after the first few days back and flung himself into a furore of activity, including the ultimate ignominy - reviewing minor poetry for the university's 'Cambridge

Review'. Before he had got as far as opening the first of seven dreary volumes of verse sent for comment, he heard that he had won a prize in one of the 'Westminster Gazette's' weekly literary competitions. His entry appeared on 2 February and a comment on it followed only five days later in the 'Cambridge Review':

Once more it is encumbent upon us to congratulate a competitor for the prizes offered in the Westminster Gazette. It is said that Brooke was successful with a translation from German to English verse; and we understand that it is the Freshman of that name, rather than the Dean, whose efforts have received appreciation.

The very next week the 'Review' published his poem 'The Call' which he later included in a volume of his poems. It reflected a love of life proper in someone still under twenty; and like this young life the poetry was not yet clarified or controlled. Not that Brooke ever came to terms with life completely, which was probably as well, or he might not have been urged on by the compulsion of conflict. Already he had the force to appreciate beauty:

> I'll write upon the shrinking skies
> The scarlet splendour of your name.

With this sense of the joyous and an almost exaggerated realism would come qualities of impishness, imagination, and controlled passion.

Next he proceeded to deal dispassionately with the six unlucky poets sent for review. One of them had actually produced two volumes of verse. Brooke sat in his study on the gloom-grey of a February afternoon reading each one conscientiously, lost to the world, and then wrote a short critical note covering all half-dozen. As this was to appear on 28 February he headed the article *'Et toute la reste'* a playful aside at the date and a polite damnation of poets who had composed such pretentious pieces as 'The New Crusade'. The same day as these reviews appeared the 'Westminster Gazette' published a prose poem 'The Five Knights', his first publicly published verse.

Mr and Mrs Brooke still grieved deeply over their

eldest son's death and when Rupert went home the next few times he took care to be even more cheerful than usual though he had felt the loss as much as them. In his letters to his cousin Erica, he said that he was puzzled about it all, felt tired and old, and did not believe in God. But he did believe in life infinitely more than most people.

With his dramatic and Carbonari activities firmly rooted, Brooke blossomed as a Fabian, too. In April he waylaid Hugh Dalton to try and convey his feelings:

'I'm not your sort of socialist,' he said with a twinkle, 'I'm a William Morris sort of socialist, but I want to join your society as an associate - if you'll have me.' This was the Cambridge University Fabian Society and Dalton said yes.

In an unpublished poem of this precise period, now mostly lost, Brooke hoped for a better world where all men should share a larger life:

> lest man go down into the dark
> with his best songs unsung.

Dalton kept a record of these lines. Almost from their first meeting he realised that Brooke was no ordinary freshman and he preserved all the letters, postcards and manuscripts from Rupert, feeling them to be important.

In view of his Liberal - and Labour - leanings, Brooke's interest in the Fabians was only logical. The fact that he had likened himself to the outlook of Morris was also in character for he felt most concerned for the creative artist and would never conform to a doctrine merely to fall in line; rather the reverse.

All this time, too, he continued to emerge as a radiant and remarkable personality. Fabianism was indirectly responsible for him meeting the four Olivier sisters, all of whom he liked. Their father, Sydney Olivier, came over to speak from Oxford, and, at a supper party afterwards, Brooke was introduced to the four girls - Margery, Daphne, Bryn and Noel. It was Noel who fell under his spell most of all, though their friendship did not develop until the following year or so as she was only an adolescent in 1907. Even at that age the memory of the fair-haired man at that Cambridge supper haunted her.

Rupert was dazzling as he pressed the girls to plates of food and hot drinks. At this particular supper in the rooms of Ben Keeling, Noel Olivier was actually less than sixteen and still at the celebrated co-educational school of Bedales in Petersfield, Hampshire. During the following few years, Rupert and Noel met many times, both in public and in secret. Later on he proposed to her ...

He entered more contests in the 'Gazette' during May and June, but although his attempts were printed neither received the prize. Then two further fragments appeared in July, one winning the prize. It was for the completion of a poem and the judges all agreed that Brooke's entry was distinctly better than the opening portion of the poem set to be finished!

Summer saw four more poems published at Cambridge under his 'scarlet spell'. After the scarlet splendour in 'The Call' two more contained references to this colour:

My song, a flame of scarlet, on your brows.

This was from 'My Song', one of three poems in the June 1907 book of King's, the 'Basileon'. It was coupled with 'Dawn' and 'The Wayfarers', the latter including the lines:

Will pale a little your scarlet lips, each mile
Dull the dear pain of your remembered face.

His down-to-earth realism appeared in 'The Dawn', written in a second-class train compartment between Bologna and Milan while returning home from Venice the previous year.

Opposite me two Germans snore and sweat
Through sullen swirling gloom we jolt and roar.

Throughout his first year at Cambridge Brooke wrote dozens, probably hundreds, of poems and then burnt most of them as soon as they were composed or after he had read them to someone.

At the end of the May term the most significant event before Brooke left on his holiday was his first meeting with Eddie Marsh. The patron from Whitehall soon saw that the poet was, in Frances Cornford's words, 'magnificently unprepared' for the humdrum life. But their friendship had to wait for Brooke was about to leave for Lulworth in Dorset with other friends. Here he lazed among the rocks and rippling waters of the Cove and thought things rather dull as he complained of a lack of promenade and pier! Nothing but the green arcs of Dorset downs sweeping to sheer white cliffs. And although he was declaring as usual that he was writing nothing, towards evening on 8 July he was stirred by the sight of pine trees silhouetted after sunset:

> Very beautiful, and still, and bending over
> Their sharp black heads against a quiet sky.

He was happy and laughed - and no longer wished to die. The poem reflected exactly his feelings at that time - the gradual eclipse of the era of 'decadence' and a move towards a freer, frank - if emotional - approach to life. Brooke hummed a song out of tune as he strode down to the village in the light of the summer moon that night. The scent of the pines followed him as he went.

The sea was encouraging a love of swimming, not one of his main interests before now, but becoming a passion in the later, Grantchester days. Next term, too, he would resume organised games though not quite with wholehearted zeal. But now it was still summer, Edwardian summer, with the drowsy sound of the sea, the lull of Lulworth.

For the lack of much else to do, Brooke read his syllabus classics and wrote and read poems. One day perched on some rocks a copy of Keats fell out of his pocket and was swept out to sea by the currents scurrying around the rocks. Brooke and a friend hopped onto a rowing boat and tracked the book down the coast till they caught it being bruised against other rocks. Brooke retrieved the volume with difficulty but it was ruined.

Years later he discovered that by an amazing coincidence Lulworth had been the last land Keats had trodden before leaving Britain forever. In September 1820, his becalmed ship stood-by outside Lulworth waiting for a wind. Keats went ashore with Joseph Severn for the day and clambered among those same rocks, before returning to the Maria Crowther to sail for Italy. Back aboard, he wrote his last sonnet starting:

Bright star! Would I were steadfast as thou art –

A year later he was dead.

For Keats, Lulworth meant the last of England; to Brooke it became a point from which he began to find himself. Despite the front of exaggerated ennui he liked to present in his letters, such as the one on attaining his twentieth birthday which had plunged him into despondency, this attitude was now not much more than a facade. Enthusiasm for life was winning over languorous cynicism. But all was not calm for the spirit of Brooke burned too bright with ecstasy to be maintained at such a pitch permanently. Meanwhile, he went back to Cambridge and the first thing he did at college was – to play football.

CHAPTER

3

Life throbbed through King's and Cambridge that autumn at an exciting, vibrant pace. The young don Bertrand Russell remembered that they were a lively group at the University during those vintage years. Rupert no longer resented the place or regretted Rugby, where every hour had been golden; in fact he developed naturally as a pivot or prominent member of every group he joined.

His legendary circle of friends began to form, for he had a talent for attracting staunch people around him. Dalton, Eddie Marsh (only occasionally seen), the Olivier girls, Frances Cornford, Geoffrey Keynes, Reginald Pole. The list was to multiply before long; now he stood on the brink of the crowded years. Brooke knew Keynes from earliest Rugby days and it was he who helped Rupert at Cambridge with translations for the contests in the 'Westminster Gazette'. Keynes also assisted by saving all his press-cuttings and contributions to periodicals, so already Keynes and Dalton were aware of his worth.

Brooke had a clear impact on Reginald Pole, who found him one of the few utterly real and rare personalities he had ever met. Pole had never known a poet to match him for simple, unaffected communication of truth, unashamed as he was of every emotion that might ripple over the surface of his mind.

This personality observed by Pole was beginning to have a vitalising effect on the Carbonari, Fabians, the philosophic Apostles, the Heretics and other societies. Yet above all other activities this term, it was drama that absorbed him most apart from pure poetry.

Dr Edward Dent, professor of music, noticed too that on his return to Cambridge after the long vacation of 1907 a new spirit seemed to be stirring there. He decided that it emanated from Rugby and Bedales. The two leaders were both, by coincidence, called Brooke: Justin Brooke hailed from Bedales and Rupert from Rugby. They were not related.

Justin, three years the elder, formed an acting group soon after term started and went along to see Rupert one evening to tell him about it.

'I remember you were in the Eumenides last year, Rupert, and seem to be keen on the theatre, so I wonder if you'd care to be a member of this new group of ours?'

'Care to? I'd love it.'

Between them they settled on a play to launch the group: Marlowe's 'Faustus'.

'Well, what shall we call ourselves?' Justin thought, 'How about the Marlowe Dramatic Society?'

The fact that Christopher Marlowe had himself been at Cambridge until 1587 appealed to Rupert, with his passion for the Elizabethan drama, and so he agreed to the title as eagerly as he accepted the invitation. Marlowe blew life, strength and everything else into tragedy, Rupert believed, and he admired the dramatist's love of the body, his passion for the world of colour and stuff, his glorious atheism.

Like all else he ever entered into, Rupert devoted his whole being to the play. When considering the casting, someone said: 'Wouldn't Rupert be right for the part of Helen?' This was followed by a deep discussion among the rest, but in the end they saw him for some reason in the darker devilry of Mephistopheles, a role as far out of character as could be conceived.

A series of secretive but excitedly enthusiastic rehearsals prepared them for the performance in the A.D.C. Theatre of the university. The mid-Edwardian audience settled into their seats after their evening meals, and looked at the programme. No names of actors appeared. An uneasy buzz of conversation went round the stalls. That was the first shock. Many more were to follow; things that seemed extra startling against the comfortingly familiar setting of the theatre, with its portraits of past personages all around the walls.

The chatter finally died down as the curtains parted on that November night. Then the older members of the audience gasped, the younger ones sat up straighter. For they saw no footlights, no scenery, nothing but a general green gloom engendered by dark velvet curtains. There was no incidental music as atmosphere. The conventional among the audience assumed a state of scandalised astonishment at the entire evening, which was admittedly unusual. Behind the stage, the cast waited pent up, and Rupert made last-minute adjustments to his cowl.

Dr Dent agreed that it was indeed a queer performance. Faustus looked absurdly young; the devil (Rupert), his face completely hidden by his cowl, generally turned his back on the audience and spoke in a thick, indistinct voice. In spite of these things, and the tedious humour of the comic scenes, the play really did have a new spirit all of its own. The tragic moments were genuinely moving. Crude, awkward and amateurish as it was, the spirit of true poetry shone through and those of the audience responsive to the idea felt that to these actors poetry was the greatest thing in life.

This, then, explained much of the reasoning behind the revolutionary staging. The group wanted to paint an impression in poetry, and to do so discarded all distractions such as scenery and music. The mood and the words were all.

But the stupefied spectators were not really impressed. This was Edwardian, not Elizabethan, England. Play presentation had 'progressed' since then. The comments in the intervals and afterwards confirmed their reaction:

'"Faustus" isn't a play at all' the elderly said, shaking their heads, 'and anyway, it was absurd for undergraduates to attempt tragedy.'

'If they were really set on it, why didn't they get somebody with experience to coach them?'

'Why do they act in the dark?'

The questions volleyed out into the night, the final words echoing distantly down the still street: 'It wasn't always in very nice taste, was it, my dear?' The crowning condemnation.

'Faustus' had been different so it must be wrong. Dr Dent and a few others saw its sincerity and he made his way backstage at the end to find the two Brookes.

'Don't worry, it had poetry and art' he told them.

'That's not what the audience thought' Rupert said.

'Never mind, you stick to your ideas and keep in touch with me. I'll expect to see something else from you soon.'

Rupert had handled the poetic passages with the true feeling to be expected but the more dramatic moments proved beyond him, and he was conscious of this as he changed from his black costume.

'He had no essentially histrionic gift, but he delivered poetry quite beautifully' Reginald Pole wrote. Yet, if Brooke's ability on stage lacked drama, the production as a whole owed a lot to his imagination behind the scenes. His forte was clearly creative rather than interpretative but he could not help wringing poetry out of a printed page.

While rehearsing for 'Faustus', Brooke did not neglect poetry, politics or the Carbonari, which added a few freshmen in October. In fact, his own outlook on the relationship between economics and the arts was actually voiced in a public lecture during November by H. Granville-Barker on Socialism and the Drama. Brooke listened to this rapt, and reported its main points for the local newspaper.

Among Granville-Barker's points were that if you 'look after the economics, the art will come of itself.' As far as Brooke was concerned, this applied to poetry, painting and all the arts just as it did to drama, and three years later almost to the day he developed his own imaginative ideas in a lecture to the Cambridge Union Fabian Society.

George Bernard Shaw visited the Fabians the same week as Granville-Barker was in the town and roused most of them there to a pitch of extreme enthusiasm with his Irish wit and passion. Brooke had yet to be convinced that he felt sufficiently in sympathy to accept the doctrines fully. Too much stress seemed to be laid on material, selfish and partisan ends, too little on pure idealism. He still saw some goodness in people politically opposed to him and he retained more tolerance of the existing order than most Fabians. Yet this was the world of the young Shaw, Wells and the Webbs, and he felt just as fervently in favour of some sort of change to the competitive, top-heavy social structure. He was probably closest in view to his uncle, Erica's father, Clement Cotterill who had just finished a social study, 'Human Justice for those at the Bottom from those at the Top'. Cotterill sent his nephew a copy of it in November and he reviewed it on publication the following May.

Wedged in amid all these activities, themselves additional to the curriculum, Brooke read and autographed in November a book by John C. Bailey on 'The Claims of French Poetry'. He furthered his acquaintance with Marot, Ronsard, La Fontaine, André Chenier, Hugo and De Lisle. This term seemed so crowded that Brooke found few days for composing verse of his own. And anything he did write he could not have considered of value, for nothing was published or survives.

Another New Year: and by mid-January Brooke was reviewing more verse and composing an occasional sonnet. One in a light vein, that month, started:

This thing must end, I am no boy!

It proceeded as a lighthearted fourteen lines of revolt on reaching the age of twenty-one, which he was due to do shortly. This he followed a fortnight later in the 'Cambridge Review' with a poem inspired by a moment that he managed to suspend, analyse and record before it dissolved. As if the world were halted for just that space of a second. It was 'In Examination' when the sun suddenly streamed in through the window of a King's room, and:

To the left and to the right,
Hunched figures and old
Dull blear-eyed scribbling fools, grew fair,
Ringed round and haloed with holy light.

The vision lasted till the light faded and they were grey again. An intriguing difference is revealed here between the date of the published poem, 20 February and that ascribed to it in the Collected Poems - 18 November the same year.

Meanwhile, like a magnet, Brooke drew around him an ever widening charmed circle of men and girls and his mind widened with it. He took people as they came and refused to be impressed by reputations. Thomas Hardy had just completed his monumental blank-verse portrayal of the Napoleonic Wars, 'The Dynasts' when Brooke ate breakfast with him one day. Rupert was very disappointed in him, for he had a thin and pessimistic voice behind a heavy moustache: a voice intoning at the inferior toast and about little else! When Brooke met Dalton and the rest next time, he told them of this depressing soliloquy on toast and things unliterary.

'We won't toast Hardy, then', a wag piped up.

The Carbonari continued to burn their charcoal at both ends. Brooke, Dalton and one or two others were generally the last to separate, often with the dawn in the sky beyond the gates of the college. Rupert would still read his latest poems to them; or they would try to thrash out the why's and woes of the world, meeting in each other's rooms.

Rupert's room, especially, had grown to mean the Carbonari meetings, for here they had their happiest nights. One particular evening they recalled from the many. Squat, intimate and sprinkled with books, the room had a lamp hanging from the ceiling, which swung slightly on the early-spring night breeze, blown via the narrow door or a window left ajar. Through one of these, too, were wafted an elusive assortment of scents and sounds from the meadows and river.

Brooke rushed around among the group, providing them with the wholesome if frugal fare of beer, bread and cheese. The excitement was rising now, for one of their current heroes had accepted their invitation. Suddenly Rupert shouted:

'Quiet - listen. Someone on the stairs.'

The next moment the door was pushed dramatically into the room and there framed in it against the darkness stood the form of Hilaire Belloc.

'Welcome to the Carbonari' Brooke called, extending a hand. And that was the signal for the start of a scintillating evening. Everyone seemed at their wittiest and four hours flashed past in an instant. Then as the great man finally left for his own room after midnight, Brooke said: 'Do come along here for breakfast if you'd like.' Belloc accepted.

After an evening like that Brooke was inclined to sleep on a bit the next morning and the following day the habit did not change. About half-past nine he stirred finally and set the breakfast in motion, then he vanished to tidy up with one of his infrequent shaves. In passing he left the front door open in case anyone arrived.

Ten minutes later Belloc strode in and with a couple of heavy steps stood towering over the frying pan in the living room where eggs and bacon were spitting away merrily. At that moment Brooke entered from the bedroom, Dalton through the front door and both of them found him sniffing the pan with a ponderous look of doubt, if not disgust!

'Don't you feel like eggs and bacon?' Rupert asked anxiously. 'If there's anything you'd rather have - '

'This will be admirable' said Belloc slowly, 'but first I'd love a tankard of audit ale!'

The beer was at once summoned, Belloc duly drained it and then they all sat down to breakfast, Belloc's seat tending to overlap the modest dimensions of the dining chair. Brooke, Belloc and Dalton eating eggs and bacon in a room of King's College, Cambridge, on a spring morning in 1908, talking over the doings of the night before.

Inspired by this visit, Brooke read a paper on Belloc to the Carbonari, complete with quotations.

On their occasional all-night sessions, a few of them would walk round the courts and beside the river for hours trying to get life clear. For they wanted, half passionately, half humorously, to sort it all out quickly. Until then, they imagined, they had been too young to think seriously; soon they might be too busy; ultimately too old. The golden time was now and they were aware of an awakening urgency as they strolled the paths surrounding the Backs while the moonlight threw soft shadows over the grass; half a dozen young men groping, grappling, seeking their own answers to the eternals.

To read poetry, write poetry, live poetry - Brooke's philosophy would keep men young always, he thought. One night, he and Dalton were sitting at a high window overlooking King's Parade. They had been discussing some point about the nature of beauty when they saw and heard some drunken members of another college going home.

Quickly Brooke said: 'Those fellows would think us very old if they had been in this room tonight, but when they go down and sit on office stools, *they* will grow old quite suddenly and many years hence *we* shall still be talking and thinking about this sort of thing, and we shall still be young'.

So there was time after all, as long as they never forgot the poetry and the wonder and avoided becoming immersed in the deadly routine of the world.

Brooke spoke with his usual infectious enthusiasm, however apparently arid the topic. Although the eternal issues might seem dry to the drunken undergraduates reeling along King's Parade, he always knew that these were what mattered most.

Rupert shared the general view of their set that it mattered immensely what was good, but comparatively little what was real. He had several fierce arguments with Dalton as to whether a man's character, as distinct from the series of states of mind through which he passed, could be good in itself; and also a controversy as to whether states of affairs, as distinct from states of mind of the persons concerned in them, could be good in themselves.

Rupert maintained that variety was good in itself. 'A world containing you and me and Maynard Keynes' he told Dalton one day, 'is obviously better than a world containing three people exactly like any of us.' (Maynard Keynes was afterwards the distinguished economist.)

Brooke never suppressed his humour, however philosophic the subject and he was always aware of the ironic in life.

'His effervescent élan always made me feel happier' Dalton told me; 'reading his letters one could almost hear him talking. And his poetry flowed forth just like live conversation - it was not forced into any special mould.'

Throughout the term, Brooke developed his attitude to the arts, propounding to the Fabians the need for artists of promise to be assured of food, fuel and clothes so that their work could proceed without wasting effort worrying over their basic livelihood. Brooke was convinced that art did not flourish in adversity, so it was up to society to see that poor but promising people were encouraged. The Fabians were interested, but their main concern lay with the living conditions of the majority, and they were less immediately absorbed with the fate of future artists.

Nevertheless, despite any difference he had with them over the emphasis of social reform he finally felt close enough to their outlook to apply for full membership. His decision was hastened by talks that spring with H.G. Wells, when the visionary Fabian visited Cambridge. Brooke made up his mind in the Easter vacation of 1908 on the way to Torquay, and told Dalton of it in a postcard from that respectable resort immediately on arrival:

April 8th, 1908 (and for 10 days)
at 3 Beacon Terrace
Torquay!

Dear Hugh,
Under the influence of a) talks with the wee fantastic Wells b) his books c) Fabian tracts d) private meditation and prayer e) arguments on the other side f-z) anything, etc, I have decided to sign even the present Fabian Basis, and to become a member (if possible) of the Central Fabian Society. The former part, I suppose, may wait till next term; as I have no Basis with me. Spiritually, the thing is done (not without blood and tears). But the latter - is it possible? What steps can I take, even now? Where write? What say? Tell me. I am eager as a neophyte always is, for action.

Yours
R

Dalton was delighted to receive this. Like many of them Brooke was falling by then under the subtle influence of the Webbs and, simultaneously, the atmosphere of Cambridge was teaching him to value and to cultivate lucidity of thought and precision of reasoning. Dalton was glad that he had seen the intellectual limitations of a 'William Morris sort of socialist' and although Rupert never studied the fine points of economics, he came to talk very good sense on the larger economic questions.

Spring came early as always to the subtropic Torquay plant life and Rupert basked in its haze of blossom and glossy leaves; after dark he looked out past the little coloured boats in harbour to the faint, flickering lights tracing the coastline to Brixham and beyond. April in

Devon, a beautiful, bitter-sweet time, with the spring sun lighting red earth, fawn sand and the sweep of the sea round the bay.

Then back to the buzz and bustle of Cambridge in late-April with bicycles beginning to fill the market square.

The editor of the 'Cambridge Review' came to Brooke for a poem to help fill the first number of the new term. He supplied 'On the death of Ta-Urt, the Hippopotamus Goddess'. Ta-Urt was re-christened Smet-Smet in the Poems of 1911.

Brooke's worth was becoming known outside the gates of King's and around this time he received an invitation to join the Apostles, a group which met once a week to discuss philosophic subjects in a not-too-stuffy way. The society was formed in 1820 - the year of Keats at Lulworth - and only one or two promising people were elected to it each year so it represented a real honour. Bertrand Russell, 15 years older than Brooke, Lytton Strachey and other prominent personalities were members. It was actually at the suggestion of Lowes Dickinson that Brooke's name had been included for election. Bertrand Russell first met Brooke through the Apostles and liked his company, recalling that he was 'loads of fun'. Russell told me this over tea and toast in his London home near the Tate Gallery.

Brooke was busier than ever this May when his sonnet 'Failure' was published. In June the 'Cambridge Review' printed 'Pine trees and sky: evening' written at Lulworth the previous summer. To the 'Basileon' for June he contributed 'Seaside'. The subject was probably Torquay with its reference to 'the friendly lilt of the band'. Here, as in another work of the period, are occasional lines of beauty which grew more frequent as he began to master the currency of poetry. For example:

The sullen waters swell towards the moon.

Brooke was occupied more with applied poetry for the rest of the term: the poetry of Milton's 'Comus'. Brooke had cherished a hope of producing it ever since 'Faustus', and he discovered the perfect excuse for performing it in 1908 - the great poet's tercentenary. Milton had studied at

41

Christ's College and so the university intended to celebrate the year. What could be more fitting than for the Marlowe Society to give 'Comus', dating from the poet's youth in 1634? Although 'Faustus' had not impressed the authorities, they relented enough to consent to 'Comus' being staged, even encouraging it.

Brooke greeted the news with wild delight, throwing a book he had been reading up to the ceiling. At once he took on the first of many tasks in connection with the performance, becoming in fact the core of the company. He repaired to room Theta of the University Library practically every day to study books on theatre construction. Moreover, he was determined to be just to Milton's memory, procuring the Trinity facsimile manuscript copy of 'Comus' to compare it with published versions for textual purity.

The group grew to include Frances Darwin (later Frances Cornford), her cousin Gwen Darwin (later Gwen Raverat) and several girls of Newnham College taking part for the first time. Brooke's charm and candour, coupled with his appearance, appealed to practically all the girls - Newnhamites, as they were known.

After he had approved the final text he became immersed in innumerable details. As artistic director of the project, he discussed with Justin Brooke ideas for costumes and then went on to evolve effects in scenery à l'avant garde Gordon Craig. For days before the play Brooke helped Albert Rutherston, the artist actually painting the scenes, by fetching pails, filling paint-pots, and in between times, supervising the direction and movement of the play - which involved also menial tasks like winding pulleys. Ultimately he created some wonderful settings using such devices as scaffold poles placed in unusual ways.

Rupert was entirely happy for a week or two, perhaps for the first time since coming to Cambridge. It was all he could do to cope with the flow of fresh jobs. He always craved for new experiences, people and places as long as he lived, and savoured them all so deeply that he was exhausted before exhausting them.

With the men all about twenty to twenty-two, and a gay group of girls to help, everyone revelled in the work.

And through it all shone the indefinable esprit of Brooke, daubing paint on the forest trees, reciting his lines lyrically, flirting with the girls. One of his helpers was Noel Olivier, now very attracted to him. One girl from the 'Comus' production had played with him in 'The Importance of Being Earnest' and he wrote to his cousin that she was very beautiful and nice and everything. And every evening they rehearsed and he had to make love to her all the time!

But 'Comus' proved more demanding than this and Rupert used his entire resources on it. They rehearsed at every odd hour they could, either in the theatre or on the lawn of a neatly walled garden with a solid summerhouse in the corner. Rupert was taking his part of the Attendant Spirit or else coaching one or more of the others. There in this old English garden the clock slipped back three centuries as they stalked about in seventeenth century clothes and Milton's words hung on the heavy summer air, until a girl's sudden laugh brought them back to reality and the modern life of 1908, with university students of both sexes audaciously acting together.

At last the rehearsals were over and it was the night of the play. Brooke's settings were remarkable, and his own portrayal more satisfactory than in 'Faustus'. Dr Dent had been following their progress with interest and, from what he had glimpsed of rehearsals, took his seat expectantly. He knew that here was to be a play of more importance to the life and growth of the participants than the audience: a work of their art and self-expression. Here is how he described the occasion:

It is difficult to criticise Comus, or to write a history of its preparation. It had much the same faults and the same merits as Faustus, though on a larger scale... Yet I feel now that anyone who remembers Comus, and remembers it with ever so slight a sense of beauty, will think of Rupert as the central figure of it; and watching rehearsals daily, as I did, I felt that, however much his personal beauty might count for, it was his passionate devotion to the spirit of poetry that really gave Comus its peculiar and indescribable atmosphere. Comus, however unimportant to the world at large, did, in fact, mean a great deal for

Rupert and his friends. It was the first time that he had had to bear the responsibility of a large undertaking and he addressed himself to it in the spirit of a scholar. It deepened his sense of poetry, of drama, and of music; it made him develop an ideal continually present in his mind, and even in later years, which gave solidity to his group - the ideal of Cambridge, of young Cambridge, as the source from which the most vital movements in literature, art, and drama were to spring.

So Milton was duly honoured in the university of his youth. Mrs Brooke came over to see the performance but as soon as she met Rupert afterwards she realised he was utterly exhausted by his mental and physical efforts and insisted on taking him home to Rugby to get over it. He protested but he was so close to a collapse that he could not really argue.

After a few days' peace he was able to write and apologise to his friends for having departed so suddenly. He could now take 'a little warm milk and Tennyson' as he sat up in bed at School Field watching one of the later cricket matches in the fixture list from the window of his room.

The muted thud of bat upon ball echoed emphasised by distant handclaps - sounds like these drifted to him as if straight from his past. Already Rugby seemed an age away though he had left it only two summers before. Now part of him belonged elsewhere and he had grown away from it in growing up. Cambridge and his contemporaries meant more, now that the adolescent phase had really ended.

As soon as he was better he said a temporary farewell to his parents again, waving goodbye to 'The Ranee' as he nicknamed his mother as he left for Rugby's mock-Gothic railway station. After this short rest he was quite recovered and found the university in its usual gaiety as end of term approached. A day or two before the long vacation actually began, with the June weather warm and set, Brooke and Dalton suggested to a couple of others from King's that it would be nice to get out of the stifling rooms and sleep out of college in the field just over the river, beyond the Backs.

So under a full moon and brittle, brilliant midsummer stars, they took food and a blanket with them, pitched camp and talked of eternity, girls and many other things. Then they settled down for an idyllic night with the elusive sweet scents of summer all around, heightened by the night. The hours passed peacefully but at first light one of the college porters espied them from the distance. They were breaking no regulations but without troubling to investigate more closely he scampered back to King's and reported to the Dean that three men and a woman were sleeping together in the Backs. Rupert wore his hair long which accounted for the error! Things were soon sorted out, however, and no penalties imposed. The four of them walked back to breakfast still roaring over their 'orgy' of three men to one girl!

Just over a month later came Rupert's twenty-first birthday and about that week he was writing 'Sleeping out: full moon'.

On 18 August Brooke wrote from his home to Hugh Dalton, about to start on a walking holiday in Wales:

Your letter is admirably precise and leaves me utterly undecided. I should love to sleep out with nothing but a few extra socks on. And yet... you in your low-lying Cambridge may not realise how cold it is o' nights - I don't know what to do. I shall do what the majority do. Tell me what the majority do. If you and Ben are passing through this city on Wednesday, you'd better drop in and take lunch here, play tennis if you like, and take me on. The invitation holds good to all Fabians who pass through, Walesward, that day. I don't know Mr. Service or his works. (Dalton had praised a Canadian poet in his letter). *I don't think I should like them. I mistrust Sourdoughs.* (The poems were called 'Songs of a Sourdough'). *What is a Sourdough? Pronounced Sour-dô or Sour-duff? Human conversations are ever inconclusive. I told my mother that the chief end of Life was Pleasure, and she burst into tears. I await your Epiphany, your bright and glorious coming with many attendant daemons, to snatch me from my drab household. My uncle the Dean will be here. No matter. It will add to the Comedy. But Ben must not be blasphemous. I told the family a lot of people would be*

*lunching here that day. 'Who and what kind?' they said.
'Oh! all right,' I vaguely smiled at them, 'practically
Liberals. There's Dalton, son of a Canon, rather a Sourdô,
you know - a Sourduff I mean. 'What's a Sourduff?' said
my mother menacingly. 'A Colonial Sentimentalist,' I said,
and drifted through Explanation for four meals... The
rumour about my age was quite true. I did it a fortnight
ago. Leaving my unprofitable Youth and its fancies, I
stepped across the Threshold of Manhood, jauntily,
manfully; leaving a company of dancing children behind.
I stumbled a little on the step which I did not perceive...*

Dalton himself could not come to Rugby on that
occasion. They did meet a month later, however, when the
famous Fabians, Sidney and Beatrice Webb, encountered
some of the Cambridge University supporters at one of the
Summer Schools. Among the group were Margery and
Daphne Olivier, two of Brooke's favourite feminine
companions.

In her diary for 15 September 1908, Mrs Webb wrote:
'The Cambridge men are a remarkable set, fervent and
brilliant.' She went on to describe Brooke as 'a poetic
beauty', though rightly judging Ben Keeling and Hugh
Dalton as the two outstanding people politically. Mrs
Webb ended another sentence in her memoir of Brooke on
that first meeting: 'This was afterwards the famous Rupert
Brooke who put me off the track by delivering a super-
conceited lecture on the relation of the University man to
the common herd of democracy.' Perhaps she mistook
Brooke's sincerity for snobbery.

Ben Keeling was certainly the leading light of the
Cambridge Fabians but the promise which Mrs Webb
noticed had no chance of fulfilment for Keeling was killed
on the Somme in 1916.

During these open-air and Summer School holidays,
Brooke and Dalton discovered the Belloc walking books
and Dalton observed how Belloc began to influence Brooke
in rhythms, just as Christina Rossetti did in muted line
endings.

The long vacation trailed into October and Rupert
spent a week or so in London putting up at the National
Liberal Club. From this address on the 7th he wrote:

Dear Hugh,
I stay here now,
I meant to say -
But you slid away -
at that thing on Sunday
This: Masterman is going to speak at Rugby and dine
and sleep at our house... so come if you like. Rugby is
hideous but you needn't notice it.

Rupert

Masterman was still a favourite young Left leader and Brooke was excited over the prospect of having him at School Field in the flesh! Dalton was able to come this time, and the day went well. Brooke and Dalton saw Masterman safely off and then Rupert suggested a look around the school. They made a tour of all the buildings and ended up in the School Chapel. Brooke pointed to the vacant space between the memorial tablets to Matthew Arnold and Clough. Half in fun, he said quietly:

'Look, they're keeping that place for me!'

Their chuckles echoed through the deserted chapel and continued across the grass to School Field. Now a tablet to Rupert Brooke in the chapel bears a profile of the poet over the complete text of his last sonnet, beginning:

'If I should die, think only this of me:'

CHAPTER
4

The first book awaiting Brooke for review on his return to King's was 'The Works of Tennyson' edited by Hallam, Lord Tennyson. Ironical in view of his recent references to warm milk and Tennyson. Somehow he could never become reconciled to the nineteenth-century romantic, and once wrote to St John Lucas from Italy that 'the only things to read this benighted place supplies are Tennyson's poems and a London Directory of 1883. I've tried both and prefer the latter!' Tennyson made him feel as if he had consumed three basins of bread and milk with too much sugar in it. Altogether Tennyson seemed doomed to be linked with milk in the mind of the passionate yet astringent Rupert Brooke.

Gradually, Brooke's work began to appear on a wider front than the 'Cambridge Review'. More intriguing than his successes of this time, however, was the publication of the poem 'Second Best' soon after it was written in the 'Mosker Books of Portland, Maine', two years prior to its English acceptance. No-one quite knows how this poem crossed the Atlantic, but probably Brooke sent it himself for, as a contemporary recalled, although Rupert's public form was the youthful poet, the real foundation of his character was a hard business faculty. This should be taken to mean efficiency rather than real commercialism, which he hated.

The theme of 'Second Best' is the eternal, one line in it urging:

Throw down your dreams of immortality.

This subject always concerned him and he tended to doubt rather than disclaim completely, insisting instead that heaven is here on earth and humanity should be what matters most. 'Our heaven is now, is won!'

Brooke loved to argue about it and one night this term

he was walking and talking with Dalton directly below Lowes Dickinson's rooms, on the top floor of Gibb's Building in the Front Court. Brooke was in the midst of making a passionate point and gesticulating emotionally when Dickinson's head, crowned with a white nightcap, popped out of the top window and called:

'I wish you'd go to bed. I can't sleep with all that chattering.'

Brooke and Dalton stopped suddenly in mid-debate, looked at each other through the gloom and chuckled guiltily as they headed for their own rooms. Next morning, they went to apologise for disturbing Dickinson.

'What were you talking about, anyway?' he asked them.

'Immortality' they said in unison.

'Now if only I'd known that, I'd have come down and joined you.' This was one of Dickinson's favourite topics too. Lowes Dickinson possessed a highly capable brain and later when Brooke heard that he had been awarded the Kahn Travelling Fellowship to widen his mind said: 'If they widen Goldie's mind any more, it'll break!' (Goldie was their nickname for Dickinson).

Brooke dashed down to London for a day or two during the Michaelmas Term and while at a Wagner concert in the Queen's Hall conducted by Henry Wood his gaze strayed over to a gross man, 'his heavy eyelids droop half-over'. Then Brooke mused on what the music meant to him, concluding that he:

likes women in a crowded place.

The poem ended on a note of fleshy realism:

his pendulous stomach hangs a-shaking.
Thus was 'Wagner' born.

Christmas came round again and as he had been working hard on his syllabus all term he felt the need of a complete change of scene and occupation. Despite this need it was with some doubts that he decided to join a party of young people bound for Switzerland and a holiday in the Alps. Here he relaxed utterly. He lived close to the crisp snows, touched by the sun into gold-glistening

49

spectrum shades, sparkling crystal-clear as the air itself. He used skis and a toboggan; caught windy winter sunlight and fell under the spell of the intoxicating, hypnotic heights - surrounding them and separating them from the rest of the real world. Or was that other world unreal, and this breathtaking beauty reality? It was difficult to decide. Hard enough to think at all, in the setting of such splendour.

The human scenery was not so bad either and he admitted that the girls in the group were better than they might have been. He was leading an almost unhealthily healthy life, eating enormously all the while.

And after days careering about on sleighs and toboggans, or slipping in the snow to joyous shrieks from the females, they all staggered, still weak from laughing, into the hotel for the evening meal and then singing and dancing. The Continental guests stared at each other in disbelief that these were the reserved Edwardian English.

A song and dance was not enough for Rupert. 'How about a play?' he suggested to them. An immediate chorus of confirmation greeted him. So they all got together to concoct a show to be presented at Christmas for the other guests staying there - whether they wanted it or not!

Rupert wrote an entire melodrama 'From the Jaws of the Octopus' which was performed for the first and final time at Klosters. His part bore the impressive label of Eugene de Montmorency. Helen Verrall, one of the Cambridge girls whom he got to know better on the holiday, portrayed his creation of the Honourable Polly Technic and among an assortment of extras were bobsleighers, skaters and private detectives. The cast, in fact, outnumbered the onlookers of this epic and everyone revelled in its climaxes.

As always the next day dawned and they had to clamber aboard the Paris-bound train, looking coal-black against its background of snow and sun.

Mentally refreshed by all this nonsense Brooke returned home to find that the two experimental choriambics he had written for the 'Westminster Gazette' had won their prize. They were published on 9 January 1909.

So the Cambridge term once more - and the Carbonari.

The survival of such a casually formed group over two and a half years of developing life at a university was really remarkable - and testimony to the flexibility of its members. Early in the term, on 5 February 1909, they assembled for their third annual dinner. The first one back in 1907 seemed far more than two years before. Now the entire strength turned out for the celebration in Rupert's rooms.

The sound of the water, lapping slightly in the night breeze, conveyed the familiar nautical air to the room, and even the light looked strangely like a hurricane lamp swaying in some cabin. Everyone was wonderfully gay, Rupert most of all. After the meal came the toasts - seven of them inscribed in a list on the menu card. And the very first, the loyal toast, turned out to be one of the shocks of the evening. It turned out to be less than loyal so perhaps the charcoal burners might have had some deep revolutionary purpose after all! Nigel Crompton looked down at his autographed menu card and read the toasts: (1) the King; (2) the Carbonari; (3) the World, the Flesh and the Devil; (4) our Better Selves; (5) Life; (6) Death; (7) the Great For-Ever. A different person proposed each one, until it came to the last, which Gerald Shove introduced. Then Rupert responded with a mellow, fluent, rambling chat, peppered with apt lines from poems. Ironic that it was he who spoke of For-Ever as he always made it clear that he had to doubt its existence.

On nights like these, the Carbonari reached its zenith as all the members became more mature. Brooke read many papers to them, but perhaps his most memorable effort was a whole epic entitled 'The Life and Death of John Rump, an English Gentleman'.

There was a prologue in heaven, when the soul of John Rump was launched for earth and then followed the ironic story of his uneventful, unprofitable life. He became a master at a public school and helped to make another generation as useless as himself. Rump was a portrait of Rupert's father. In due time Rump died and the epilogue - like the prologue - was staged in heaven. Rupert was working himself up now to a frenzy of enthusiasm and he rounded it off with a superb and angry dialogue between John Rump and the Almighty. He alternated the voice with more and more difficulty as the argument heightened but finally Rump won the day and Heaven vanished in a high wind.

'Bravo! That was terrific, Rupert,' one of them called as he came to his last line and grinned. Dalton patted him on the back too. The original paper is probably lost but Dalton always kept a copy of the death scene and the epilogue.

As winter passed Brooke began to be drawn towards an outdoor life. Switzerland still lingered in his soul as did the seaside summer holidays. He took advantage of an early Easter to spend a short holiday at Beckey Falls in North Devon where he indulged in chest expansion exercises and rambles over the hills in a combined attempt to develop his already presentable physique.

The house had a panorama ranging from the nearby grass and spring flowers of the garden to the Falls, forest and hills, silhouetted on a skyline of pastels washed pale after the westerly winds and rain. Despite the mixed March weather he relished this course of nature in which he also prescribed a vegetarian diet, few clothes, cold baths and hard work. His studies were for the classical tripos due to be taken in June. He was really working for it now and had set his mind on getting it if possible.

Brooke was beginning to look at himself and his life quite seriously now. But what were other people thinking of him? Someone in 'The Meteor' thought that during this 1906-09 period he had sometimes been slightly cynical, intolerant and petulant - characteristics almost to be expected of a brilliant and admired undergraduate.

A more balanced judgement is given by Eddie Marsh who found him 'self-examining and self-critical to the last degree, but hardly ever self-absorbed.' By Frances Cornford: 'endlessly kind in helping me with my verses.' By Mrs Asquith: 'he was noticing all the time... and he seemed never to forget the smallest detail.' And by J. T. Sheppard: 'he was sensible enough and strong enough to take flattery, in the long run, for what it was worth; and he valued the affection that was critical, not flattering.'

The magic of May week assumed a special radiance in 1909 as it marked the meeting of Rupert Brooke and Henry James, 'as if patriarch greeted neophyte'. The two men met amid the glory of Cambridge when fashion, beauty, talent and manhood mingled with spring and summer at its most exquisite moment, transforming the shops and the streets, the colleges, meads and river into a week of wonderland out of the measure of time.

While some people maintained that Rupert always acted entirely unselfconsciously, others claimed that he was aware of the self-image he might be projecting for any given occasion. He was said to vary it according to the person and place. As Timothy Rogers reminds us about this initial meeting with Henry James, Rupert remarked: 'I did the fresh boyish stunt, and it was a great success!'

Henry James found Rupert 'a creature on whom the gods had smiled their brightest.' It was at King's, he recalled, 'during a short visit there in May week, or otherwise early in June 1909, I first, and as I was to find, very unforgettingly met him. He reappears to me as with his felicities all most promptly divinable, in that splendid setting of the river at the Backs; as to which indeed I remember vaguely wondering what it was left to such a place to do with the added, the verily wasted, grace of such a person, or how ever such a person could hold his own, as who should say, at such a pitch of simple scenic perfection.'

James became aware too of Brooke's 'irony, his liberty, his pleasantry, his paradox' for 'the medal of the mere pleasant has always a reverse for him'. This was completely true, confirmed by Brooke's own admission that intense surroundings or feelings often moved him to write in opposite vein. Although extremely emotional, he was never swamped by sentiment but could spice it with another mood to give extra point and piquancy by contrast.

The last weeks approached before sitting the tripos, yet a steady stream of poems were despatched to the 'Saturday Westminster' which more often than otherwise won the prize in the contest set. Among these light offerings was 'a pritty lamentable ditty of love's flighte'.

To the 'Basileon' for June 1909 Brooke contributed the sonnet 'Day and Night' while in the same magazine, that humorous yet pathetic man, Arthur Schloss, gave a vivid cameo of the Carbonari as they might relax after their many mental exertions among literature and the arts:

"Following the excellent example set by the Chetwynd Society, the Carbonari have also decided to give a ball. 'It is beginning to be realised' said Mr Dalton in an interview with our representative, 'that the waltz and polka are an inadequate expression of the rhythmic emotions. We have arranged that our programme shall contain several innovations. I myself shall cantilate "Whitman" while striking a three-stringed lyre and performing harmonic gyrations.' Other items of less importance will be as follows: Mr Reitlinger, a noted disciple of la Belle Duncan, will give a series of classical dances. Mr Baker, his recorded prestissimo Jig for which he has been training since April. Mr Shove will dance to the music of Gluck's newly discovered opera, 'Le Roi aux Enfers'. Mr Ricard will croon folk songs to a minuet step, in sandals and a sombrero. Mr Shand will sway to a 'mouvement decadent' by Jules Hippolyte Montmartre (as discovered by the late Queen). Finally Rupert Brooke will perform a dream-dance on tiptoe!"

The Carbonari had burned bright, never more so than now, but as June, the exams and the third year all ended, they decided to let it die. It had had a good life, Brooke thought, and they did not want to risk spoiling the memory by allowing it to live too long. In one way their last meeting marked a sad moment, but it also meant they had grown up since the autumn of 1906 and recognised the need and inevitability of change in themselves and their lives. In any case this particular evening was a perfect summer scene and the Carbonari would always stay in their memory as an integral part of their years of youth.

Having taken this course they broke up the last meeting early, with handshakes all round. Brooke wandered off among the stone buildings, serene and still in the gold-tints of sunset. The first star shone in a deepening blue sky as he stopped by the Backs to look and listen. This was the magic moment of the day anywhere on earth but at Cambridge, with its chimes and timelessness, it was touched with unreality. The zenith, when one could burst with the beauty of it all.

Brooke let the day die all around him and settle into a midsummer dusk before he strolled back to his study, pushed the latticed window further open and wrote the two words 'Blue Evening' on a scrap of paper. When he went to bed at last he had written the whole poem starting:

> The straight grey buildings, richly dimmer,
> The fiery windows, and the stream
> With willows leaning quietly over,
> The still ecstatic fading skies...

Here was a turning point, he knew, as the third year finished. The long vacation always conveyed the sense of coming change and this time it was more so than ever.

Next day Brooke quickened his walk to get to the notice board where the results of the classical tripos would be posted. This was silly, he told himself, hurrying like an eager schoolboy. He had to know and in a few minutes he did. He had missed a first but there was his name safely among the second-class honours: R.C. Brooke. A moment of resentment and then he shrugged his shoulders and went off in search of Dalton.

Already he and Hugh Dalton had decided that after three years of being confined in college they had not been as brilliant as they ought, so were resolved to move out of King's the following term to detach themselves from the eddying currents of Cambridge which had apparently absorbed too much of their energies.

Dalton handed him a cup of coffee. Brooke thanked him, asking 'Where will you go, Hugh?'

Dalton considered as he stirred in his sugar.

'To Newnham, I think. And you?'

'I don't quite know yet, but I've the urge to try and find somewhere at Grantchester. It's just far enough out of town.'

'Well, I hope you do.'

After the coffee Dalton finished his packing for the vacation and some of the others came in to collect him for the train.

'I'll come along and see you all off,' Rupert offered. Then, as the train wrenched itself out leaving a fog of smoke scurrying along the platform, Brooke darted back to King's for lunch.

Another lovely day and the rest of it to do as he liked. He thought over his idea of Grantchester and suddenly made up his mind to go there in the afternoon. He had an address of someone who might be able to put him up next term.

As soon as lunch was over he set out to stroll through the meadows to the village. Most people had left college already and a silence hovered all around. He left the crenellated block of King's in the drowsy early afternoon. On the other side of the court prickly pinnacles pointed into a haze-hot sky and the figures on the clock shone bronze in the sun. Green grass with the sun on old stone, the central arch framing a glimpse of the Backs sloping slightly towards the water.

King's Parade led into Trumpington Street, then a right turn to the narrows of Silver Street. He glanced down Queen's Lane for a last view of King's for an hour or two. Over the bridge he walked up to the junction with Newnham Road, a reminder that his path and Dalton's were already parting a little. Brooke strolled past the row of tall, early-nineteenth-century dwellings on the left and smiled at the Malting House with its one oast alongside - one of the familiar landmarks on this road. Crossing to the meads he saw the miniature falls of the river clogged with reeds. The riverside path followed the winding water, while poplars dotted the meadows with measured elegance. Branches bowed across the river, their tips almost meeting in the high-summer bloom. Chattering, fluttering crows sat dark against the sun in the treetops. Brooke breathed in deeply.

Back to the road for a few minutes, past a row of red villas, lately built, leading to Grantchester Meadows. Away on the left rose more regal poplars, and the Granta reached the meadows proper by a sharp bend, where two willows stirred the surface of the water.

Brooke looked straight ahead along the earthy path, and there, a mile off, nestled Grantchester church, trees clustering round its tower. Little inlets from the river wound to the edge of the footpath, running a hundred yards or so from the main stream. The sun glinted through laden boughs as a flock of birds swept westward. His eyes followed them for a moment till they veered out of sight. A row of tiny terraced houses heralded the beginnings of Grantchester on the road from Cambridge.

On the whim of the moment he stopped, turned round and walked backwards for a few yards watching the spires of the city retreating. His shadow fell dark over the lush green grass as the sun turned bonfire smoke to gold. The root of a nearby tree, jutting through the path, almost tripped him up, bringing him back to awareness again. He turned round to face the right way and sauntered on across the meadows till the river ran away in the distance and the path led to the heart of Grantchester opposite the church. His eyes took him into its bounds, not for religious reasons but for the sense of peace pervading it.

He had passed the church several times before but hadn't realised that its records went back to 1280. The decorated Gothic chancel had been built in the mid-fourteenth century, the 56-foot tall tower a little later at the end of that century. The western afternoon light brought the stained glass to life with its portrayals of St. Peter, St. Andrew, St. Paul and, at the back, Bede, Wycliffe and Tynedale. A shaft of sunlight suffused dark red by one of the windows fell at an angle across the church till it was broken by the back of one of the middle pews. Rupert walked around the interior, paused at the pulpit and then moved back along the aisle. He found the atmosphere intensely restful although he had little sympathy with the teachings of the church itself.

Out in the open again, he followed the road along to The Orchard, the house where he had heard there might be accommodation. Its sash windows, neat paint work and white-washed walls appealed to him, and he sought out the lady in charge, a plump and weatherbeaten woman who succumbed inevitably to Rupert's radiant manner. He had soon arranged to stay there and she showed him the room he would occupy, opening on to a creeper-covered veranda and looking over an old-English rose garden.

With that settled he waved her a cheery farewell and continued his exploration. He thought of taking the path opposite the house to Barton and Haslingfield - the names sounded so intriguing - but decided instead to leave that for another day and to go on towards the mill. Brooke passed the orchard that gave the house its name and blended into the meadow beyond and the quiet little cottage of Yew Garth, home of Professor Cecil Warburton.

At the Old Vicarage he cast a casual look before proceeding to the pool below the mill.

There, in the midsummer mid-afternoon, he thought of the medieval church and then of Chaucer in this very village writing 'The Miller of Trumpington'. His mind flowed on, like the water gurgling below the bridge, to the nineteenth century and Byron.

'Byron was a lodestar to Brooke' Bertrand Russell said to me. And strangely Byron was at Cambridge and Grantchester exactly a century before Brooke. He had been born 99 years earlier than Rupert and, like him, died among the Greek islands.

Brooke sat on a stone wall and gazed into the pool. What a wonderful day. Here was history, poetry and the essence of England at her best. Here at the heart of culture in Cambridge. This was an afternoon to be remembered, when he first met Grantchester on intimate terms. What Rugby had been until 1906 and King's till 1909, Grantchester was to become for the next three or four years - and in a symbolic way for the rest of his life. He sensed it first on this day by the mill.

There was no point in delay so after a return to Rugby to see his home he moved his things into The Orchard. He had scarcely settled there when he left it for August and most of September, first to re-join his parents at a house in Clevedon on the Bristol Channel.

With their agreement, Rupert issued invitations to most of his friends to come down there during the summer. Eddie Marsh was one who accepted, though their friendship was yet to develop.

Rupert had been seeing Noel Olivier on and off for two or three years now and Mrs Brooke was beginning to believe he felt seriously about the girl, who was still quite young. When he went to his mother to tell her whom he wanted to invite to Clevedon, she said:

'Yes, you can invite the Oliviers, if you want to, Rupert, but not that young one!' Despite this he continued to see Noel, either at the Oliviers' home in Limpsfield, Surrey or at holiday parties or elsewhere.

Dalton also accepted the Somerset invitation. While he and a few others were down with Rupert they decided one day to write and invite Ramsay Macdonald to Clevedon

58

with them. The letter was despatched within the hour but although they knew he was at his home he never answered their joint invitation. Dalton gave him a bad mark for this but no-one really missed him.

After Clevedon, Brooke and Dalton joined four other Fabians at the summer school in North Wales for a few days where the Webbs were presiding. It was still summer and spirits ran as high as the temperature. At one stage a member of the group was found by the Webbs locked outside on a ground-floor balcony of the house - in company with a chamber pot! The Webbs were not at all amused at this horseplay which they felt both unedifying and immature. When the luckless person was finally let indoors the whole younger set collapsed on their beds to the accompaniment of various comments pertaining to the vessel!

Mrs Webb found the talks they all had interesting but thought that they did not want to learn. She concluded that the egotism of the young university men was colossal and wondered if they were worth bothering about. She had failed to appreciate that it was a vacation - the summer one, too - and these men were still pretty young. Brooke and Dalton, for all their wit and wisdom, had only celebrated their respective twenty-second birthdays a week or two earlier.

While the fun was going on in Wales, the September number of the 'English Review' appeared with four of Brooke's poems including 'Blue Evening' and 'Finding'.

Norman Douglas was on the staff of this periodical in 1909 and during the earlier part of the vacation met Brooke three or four times at the office. Douglas liked his work more than most which they received for consideration but did not fall under the Brooke personal spell so much as many others. Indeed Douglas felt, rightly or not, that if the two of them were ever left stranded on a desert island sooner or later they would come to the end of their conversational tether. For Douglas admitted that he liked someone he could dislike - or with whom he could quarrel! There was no disliking Brooke, he felt, nor was quarrelling possible with a supremely contented man.

Douglas did not regard Brooke's poetry of that time as outstanding but would describe it as possessing a breezy obviousness. Brooke was a dear, transparent, social creature. Nevertheless he had a spine and was vertebrate. Douglas saw the Brooke of summer 1909 as a man with a positive gift of yea-saying to life: assimilative, zestful, unafraid of realities.

The editor of the 'English Review', Austin Harrison, revealed extreme indecisiveness about accepting poetry submitted by some of Brooke's contemporaries and Rupert himself. One unfortunate contributor actually died while waiting for Harrison to make up his mind about a poem. And one of James Elroy Flecker's best poems - either 'The Golden Journey to Samarkand' or 'Gates of Damascus' - reposed for a long time before being finally rejected. Flecker was consumptive and poor so a small cheque could have helped him a lot.

'Blue Evening' and the three others by Brooke were accepted. The vacation ended. Then a day or two after the start of term he ran into Dalton in Cambridge. Both of them were now out of college, Brooke at Grantchester, Dalton reading economics at Newnham.

Just as they met, some of the year's freshmen floundered past them into King's.

'Don't these young men make you feel old?' Dalton asked Rupert in mock earnest.

'No' he said, 'not old, only tremendous!'

They had come quite a way since that first Sunday when they met on the steps of the provost's lodge three years ago - two fellow freshmen.

CHAPTER

5

'My dear chap' Rupert greeted an old friend in the university, 'I did not really begin to live till I went out of college. You can picture me leading the rustic life, broken by occasional visits to Cambridge; keeping poultry and a cow; playing simple tunes on a pan pipe; bathing every evening at sunset; and taking all my meals in a rose garden!' This should all be taken with some salt to allow for Brooke's naturally extravagant expression but it was still clear that here was a way of living he liked.

His verse began to develop. H. W. Garrod has said that Brooke began to be a great poet when he got away from Cambridge. Garrod accounts for some half a dozen worthwhile poems of the Cambridge period ending in the summer of 1909 and these were only written by running away from the people who admired him, by getting clear of Cambridge. Except for this number, nothing he wrote inside college equals almost anything outside. It is amazing how little Brooke was spoilt considering how much he was feted by his contemporaries. His character could so easily have been ruined.

Meanwhile, although his verse matured, it was not at the expense of other activities he considered really important. From The Orchard that autumn he wrote to a Miss Garrett in Girton about a meeting with the Webbs, in a hasty handwriting:

I am enclosing a notice of the Webb meeting on Thursday. If there's any place in Girton where such a thing may be posted, can you put it up? As you see, it's not an exclusively Fabian thing, and other people may like to go. If any dons or elderly people that you hear of, who are interested in Poor Law Reform, want to go, I will send you reserved seats for them if you let me know how many. There will only be a few rows reserved: and only for such people.

It may be very full.

Brooke's illuminating personal letters were multiplied by many more such official notes as these. Sybil Pye recalls that in one of their discussions the phrase 'an artistic eye in a business head' caught Brooke's attention; he said he believed the combination was possible and he certainly aimed at making it so. She was sure he had a happy talent for organization.

This immediate post-graduate era was when Arthur Benson, master of Magdalene College, knew Brooke best: never intimately but quite well. Here is his recollection:

My impression of him is vivid and clear, which is hardly to be wondered at, for he was very unlike other people. His charm, his enjoyment of life, his great personal beauty, the imperishable quality of some of his poems, and the strange suddenness of his death have combined to create a sort of legend about him, and to invest him with a mysterious sanctity which would both have amazed and amused him - and vexed him. For he has become not a very animated and actual human being, but a figure like Linus or Hylas or Lycidas, solemnised by the shadows of his untimely death. Yet the very existence of this legend, with its enfolding rarity, is of itself abundant testimony to the high and abiding quality of his charm and his work.

An enthusiastic undergraduate talked to me about him with generous and overwhelming enthusiasm, and indeed had made it his business to collect Rupert's fugitive verses. Later he brought me a packet of these to see. I own I did not think them greatly promising - conventional in their deliberate modernity, uneven, and bizarre. Then I met him in the rooms of another undergrad. He strolled in very late. He was far more striking than exactly handsome in outline. His eyes were small and deeply set, his features healthily rounded, his lips frank and expressive. It was the colouring of face and hair which gave a special character. The hair rose very thickly from his forehead, and fell in rather stiff, arched locks on either side - he grew it full

*and overlong. It was a beautiful dark auburn tint inclining
to red, with an underlying golden gleam in it. His
complexion was richly coloured and his face much tanned,
with the tinge of a sun-ripened fruit.*

*He was strongly built, but inclined to be sturdy and
even clumsy, rather than graceful and lithe. His feet and
hands were somewhat large, and set rather stiffly on their
joints. His hands had no expressiveness or grace. Nor did
he sit or move with any suppleness, but lounged or rather
huddled in his chair...his glance and regard were frank and
friendly. He was thought to have a real critical gift and
considerable erudition. But he was impatient of college
restraint and lived often at Grantchester, working, bathing
and exploring the country on foot or with a bicycle. He
came to dinner with us.*

*I don't remember his saying anything markedly
memorable, but just joined in the talk in a lively and
companionable way. When he went away, we agreed that
he was not in the smallest degree spoilt by all the attention
and adoration he received, but was living a tough,
enthusiastic life with strong preferences, and without any
pose. He had no touch of intensiveness, of affectation.
After this I came to know him better. One day he came
dressed in a coal-black flannel shirt with a bright red tie
and a suit of grey homespun.*

The Michaelmas term passed, with Brooke working
hard for the Charles Oldham Shakespeare Prize which he
won in December. Christmas came round again and
another party was being organized for Switzerland which
he joined with more readiness than last time.

Brooke could recapture every emotion from ecstasy to
despair and the rough crossing to France on a late
December day inspired another of his intense,
'objectionable' pieces, 'A Channel Passage' which ended
with this tongue-in-cheek rhyme:

And still the sick ship rolls. 'Tis hard, I tell ye,
To choose 'twixt love and nausea, heart and belly.

Earlier reference to brown gobbets and sobs and
slobber were judged offensive by some select circles: even

Eddie Marsh found them unnecessarily unpleasant.

Rupert travelled with old friends - Dudley Ward, Jacques Raverat and Daphne and Margery Olivier. Helen Verrall came too and she assisted him with what threatened to become an annual event for the other visitors to the hotel: the dramatic offering.

'Let's have something musical this year' Rupert suggested. 'I know, how about a comic opera?'

Helen beamed at this brainwave. Brooke at once set about composing a libretto, fitting light verses to existing music such as the 'Soldiers' Chorus' from 'Faust'.

'It's going to be called "The Super-Ski"' he announced next day with mock importance, 'and we'll all have to wear ski-suits. And another thing. I can't sing, so someone will have to provide a voice from the wings while I mime my part'. Dudley and Jacques both offered to do this and eventually all the characters were allotted.

After a few evenings' rehearsal, New Year's Day was chosen as a fitting day for the final performance, which went with a fine swing from first chorus to last. The reception from the foreign guests was, as previously, one of tolerant indifference deteriorating towards actual aggression as the essentially English humour of Rupert's lyrics was lost on them.

The next morning the faded lounge still showed evidence of 'The Super-Ski' even after they had all left on the first stage of their journey home. Brooke accompanied them but was suffering from minor poisoning through bad water. He did not say much about it as they stopped for several days at Basle and Paris to view paintings and other sights, yet all the time he was staggering round with a temperature, feeling miserably ill. Luckily, the Channel crossing was calmer and at last he got back to Rugby after what seemed endless days of trailing around Europe.

At once he sank into bed, still with a temperature, but his own illness paled before the news awaiting him at home: his father had just had a minor stroke and was being taken to London to consult a specialist. The trip proved futile for the doctor could neither comfort nor treat him much. Back at School Field, Rupert was recovering from 'flu which followed his poisoning but he realised he could not leave his mother at the moment until things changed.

The Orchard, Grantchester. Rupert moved to this idyllic cottage from Cambridge in the autumn of 1909. From the author's collection.

Overleaf: Breakfast with unknown companions in the garden of The Orchard, Grantchester in 1909. From the author's collection.

Although not selfish by nature he was appreciating how much more Grantchester meant to him than Rugby.

Following his practice of writing in opposite vein to any intense prevailing mood, he passed a convalescent day on 11 January composing a light love-piece looking back at 'The One before the Last'.

how faded dreams of Nineteen-ten
were Hell in Nineteen-five.

This he followed with two sonnets more in the mood of the cloud-filled sky behind the empty school buildings opposite.

Rupert had not long to wait for a change in the situation. A few days later his father suffered a second stroke and died. School Field suddenly seemed cold and even more empty. No voices of juniors broke its chilly passages and rain drooped down the window panes. Despite John Rump and all he had thought of his father, Rupert felt an intense sense of tragedy, similar to the days following his brother's death.

To add to it all, Mr Brooke was buried on the same day that the boys trooped back to School Field from their Christmas holidays. The news buzzed round in a moment and small groups of boys stood huddled in various parts of the house or garden throughout the day. Rupert helped his mother survive the funeral but the shock had been severe to her. Then he went down again with a further bout of influenza. He lived through a concentrated few days of depression but because of their intensity and his unquenchable verve he bounced back to life determined to save his mother having to move house, at least temporarily.

'I'm all right now, mother, and I've had an idea. I'm going to take over as housemaster tomorrow. I'll see the head and try to arrange it at once.'

The head agreed readily to this measure and so Rupert stayed the entire Easter term of ten weeks as acting housemaster at School Field. In a week or two he recovered his spirits completely and was surprised to discover himself a good master with a bluff Christian tone that was wholly pedagogic, as he put it to a friend. He received respect, too, as the seniors still remembered him from their 1905-06 days and how he represented the school 'at various violent games'. He in his turn genuinely liked the 53 boys under his care, although he could not bear to think that they would inevitably follow the well-worn convention to Cambridge and ultimately take their unimaginative place in the upper classes of the country. This was what made teaching at public school intolerable for him: the system of snobbery which moulded most of them into the reverse of individuality. His Fabian feelings reached their strongest this year.

Cambridge was all right as long as you were aware of its dangers and kept clear of that fatal mould of mediocrity. Meanwhile what he would be missing there this term came home to him when he contributed an article on 'Richard II' to the 'Cambridge Review', preceding a performance to be given by the Marlowe Society. He was sick to miss this he told Frances Cornford. By compensation he gained a sense of self-reliance through his term at Rugby. It widened his sphere of experience still more. Across these three months he had been writing 'Dust' which he completed at the same time as his locum was over.

In April Brooke bade a final goodbye to School Field as he helped his mother move into a small, uninteresting house in Bilton Road, Rugby, with only a number to mark it from other identical dwellings on each flank. The term had been stimulating in one way, but now he realised afresh the significance of his father's death - he would never see School Field again. From now on it was Bilton Road. Even the name seemed to reflect its lack of individuality. How could you get out of the rut of routine in a road like that?

With Mrs Brooke safely installed she insisted that he took an Easter holiday, his first relaxation from strain since that operatic evening on New Year's night.

Once more at Lulworth, he tramped across the Downs and breathed the south-west spring wind which smoothed the short grass in its path. South, nothing but sun and sea; north, cottages nestling in the Dorset dales. Everywhere the rugged, ragged grandeur of Purbeck stone homes and in the distance the outline of Corfe Castle.

Here he forgot that, from now on, there would be no

tennis court at home, that he had no father and had lost one brother. Before lunch he read Elizabethan plays at the rate of twenty a week and then in the afternoons he clambered up the cliffs to sort them all out in his mind. Three a day was quite an average to assimilate. This work on the Elizabethans went towards the Harness Prize Essay. In one provocative mood he declared with the exaggeration known so well to his friends, that the only good plays written between 1500 and 1650 were 'The Faithful Shepherdess' and perhaps 'Anthony and Cleopatra'! The mood of the moment, sincerely felt, but not to be taken too seriously as lasting dramatic criticism. His essay won the prize later in the year under the title 'Puritanism as represented or referred to in the early English drama up to 1642'.

Probably at Lulworth, too, he wrote one of the best of his sonnets, 'The Hill', notable among other things for a poignantly perceptive last line:

And then you suddenly cried, and turned away.

Lulworth was doing Brooke a lot of good. One day during the Rugby term he had gone to see Arthur Benson at Cambridge and talked with occasional animation, interspersed with moods of depression.

'My mind has become stuffy and unreliable' he told Benson; 'I feel I want to meet strangers and get a current of new thoughts and images'. Lulworth was the first step in this direction.

Back at Cambridge the two men dined together again and Benson noticed that Brooke seemed infinitely better, even more handsome and charming. They talked discursively about books and Brooke laughed at his host's humorous tales, conveying to Benson nothing of the typical intellectual. He was easily pleased in life, Benson thought, and observed how Rupert preferred the talk to wander where it would.

At the end of April, with Grantchester garlanded in early apple blossom, Brooke went back there for the first time that year. He said he wanted to see the spring coming to the village and arrived at its height. What was the idyllic influence the place offered? A timeless tranquillity?

Grantchester had a shy, evasive beauty; an unmistakable though not exceptional charm. Rupert discovered it more and more as the weeks went by.

Behind the church stood an old manor house comfortably embedded in trees; and there the road turned at a sharp angle by a mossy wall of mouldering brick, and followed the line of the fosse of the Roman camp which gives its name to the place. On the left, a little lower down, the Old Vicarage, a house of ancient red brick. A big garden behind it, fringed by great chestnut trees, ran down to the river. Here, in a straggling wilderness, was a rockery of ecclesiastical fragments and a ruinous old building of clunch and tiles, designed as a garden-house but with an excrescence like an apse which gave it the air of having been intended, in a rococo manner, to present the appearance of a chapel or oratory.

Pursuing the main road, zigzagging with extraordinary pertinacity, Brooke used to pass a pleasant, tiled, orange-plastered house in an ample garden, which cheered him invariably with its warm Mediterranean colouring. The road came out by Grantchester Mill, passing between the mill and the pool.

This was not the mill made famous by Chaucer's tale - the ruins of that stood farther up the stream - but a modern structure whose actual mill kept grumbling and groaning while the stream spun and gurgled into the deep pool; floating off among green meadows and under high, dark-shadowing chestnuts into a wide and glimmering reach of water.

Rupert found that the mill-leat embraced a broad islet, deep in meadow grass on either side of the road and all enclosed by towering elms, the wilderness of Trumpington Hall and the dark shadowy groves that brood over Byron's Pool.

Arthur Benson loved this spot, too, recording that 'in a day of high summer you could hardly find a sweeter place; all embowered in branching trees and close-set orchard; the fowls picking up the fallen grain; the lazy anglers by the stream; the deep-brimmed pool with the breaking bubbles and the darting fish; the fragrant, fresh, weedy scent, and the distant clink of rowlocks over the grass. A dreaming charm...'

The gracious Granta winding through the woods; wistaria-clad houses on a lowly hillock; blossom moving magically in a spring sunset - these are the things which cannot change.

Grantchester had peace too. There was just one cab, to be hired for weddings or funerals, driven by a coachman whose top hat was a tempting target for stones in summer, or winter snowballs. Dick Cox, the village carrier, smoked his pipe while his pony lolled along at leisure.

Then there were the village simpletons. Alf was lame and cross-eyed, yet walked to Cambridge each day to take up his post as crossing sweeper along the road by the Backs. His crony was called Spider Riddle, for his tall, spindly appearance. These two often quarrelled, to the gentle amusement of the villagers. They would shout abuse at one another and aim wild blows through the air - but both were afraid to come close enough to risk being hit! Then the deep peace returned to Grantchester.

Brooke moved enchanted through this reverie of 'apple blossom and the river and sunsets' but still managed more or less daily touch with Cambridge. He was elected president of the Fabians and in a room of Gibbs' Buildings at the south-west corner of the front court they would all foregather for socialism, beer, bread and cheese. Another activity later this summer was to be a repetition of 'Faustus', while yet a further group enlivened by the twin spirits of Brooke and Dalton was the Fish and Chimney, where plays of all periods were read and discussed.

Brooke found himself busier than ever, cycling to and from Cambridge, or entertaining his host of friends out at The Orchard. Several of the university people also lived at Grantchester, including the sisters Sybil and Margaret Pye who often walked down the road from their own home to visit Brooke at the guest house.

One evening while Rupert was reading poetry to them and some others, the scents of spring pervading the room - coupled to Brooke's mellifluous delivery - prompted Margaret to make a delightfully spontaneous sketch of him as he spoke. On the back of the paper she drew another, more fanciful, impression of him supposedly drinking Dudley Ward's health in the latter's rooms at St John's

College.

The Pye girls became close friends of Brooke during this year and next. As the days stretched longer and longer they talked to him of everything under the summer sun and Sybil made mental memories of each golden day. Rupert had this capacity with everyone - of making them feel that the place and the time were both special, that this was a moment for which they had been born.

Sybil loved talking to him for she had never known so sympathetic a conversational opponent. He had a way of working her opinion into his reply so that his dissension seemed merely a comment on some conclusion already reached! The result of his natural kindness and innate sense of good manners.

At other times he would sit in silence among a group, looking from speaker to speaker till they thought he had wandered far from their present themes; but a quick comment or question, with a sudden intenseness in his look, showed a mind awake and aware.

Occasionally his abstraction did go deeper. A group of them, including the Pye girls, were in the middle of a favourite game of the day, Up Jenkins, in which someone had to try and point out a sixpence hidden beneath one of the other's hands. It came to Rupert's turn to order all hands to be laid palm downwards on the table. Then, instead of proceeding to guess which one concealed the coin, he just sat looking distantly at them till good-natured shouts of impatience echoed down the line of players. Suddenly, smiling in half-apology, he jerked himself to consciousness and explained:

'Oh, but hands are so beautiful!'

Brooke was normally much more practically aware than this, though, and had a strong capacity for organising not only business but social affairs as well. One day during the May Week of 1910, three separate parties fell on the same day, and as everyone was anxious not to refuse any one of them, the three festivities were combined to meet in the Pye's garden.

There was clearly a danger here, for among the mutual acquaintances a number did not know each other. The task of trying to merge such diverse elements into anything approaching a sympathetic social entity seemed so hard as to be not worth attempting; but Rupert thought otherwise. In fact by his very presence, by moving from group to group he dissolved their incongruities and created links. The contrast of his conspicuously attractive appearance and his unobtrusive manner stamped the scene with an atmosphere hardly any of them forgot. His sincere interest in everything was quickly catching so that lively conversation soon superseded the conventional commonplaces which had threatened to dampen the entire affair. Brooke knew them all and liked them all. That was his unconscious outlook on life.

With June joyfully launched by the celebrations of May Week, Brooke took every advantage of the summer. On most days he swept up an armful of books into a canoe moored behind The Orchard and just let it drift along, with only his left hand dangling a paddle through the water. As the boat glided beneath the branches, seen again in the glass-still stream, he made rapid, jerky notes from books on any scraps of paper available and whether alone or accompanied he read out random passages to enjoy the sound of the forms and cadences. Spenser, Ben Jonson, Beaumont, Fletcher and Webster all seemed to receive an added grace when heard here, among the dark reflected trees and the sudden wide openings across the flat, heat-misty meadows.

Often he paused at one particular open space. The proportions of the trees that bounded it and the pale far-running distance between made it seem to him a happy setting for a play he would write. Here Rupert sat superbly suspended among serene depth and shadowed height.

He came to know each curve of the course the river took, each tree-clump that marked it with an uncanny intimacy. Sometimes he brought the Pye girls home by river from Cambridge after an evening event. Coming up with him in a canoe those three miles to Grantchester on a dark starless night, this intimacy was startling. Every possible landmark seemed merged in a blanket of black and even the water-surface ceased to show the faintest gleam, meeting its muffled banks invisibly and unheard. Except for the soft splash of the paddles they might have been floating in some totally new medium, free of boundaries, out of all reach, in a fourth dimension.

Nevertheless Brooke kept on course. He knew, he told Sybil and Margaret, when they were nearing home by the sound of a certain poplar that grew there - for its leaves rustled faintly even on nights like this. The girls peered at each other, then out into the dark and only half-believed him; so many poplars rose by that river and it sounded absurd of Rupert to be able to recognise one. Yet he was right. At a certain point, there was the slightest sound of leaves stirring on the suggestion of a breeze. Rupert shipped his paddle for a second to hear.

'Listen! There it is - can you hear?'

And sure enough, he landed them without hesitation at Grantchester by their own garden, mooring the canoe as easily as if it were midday.

On another afternoon he picked them up and they tied the canoe to a tree trunk while they sat on the river bank. Rupert started to give the British poets marks according to his view of their worth. He was enjoying himself tremendously but when it came to awarding Wordsworth only a low rating, Sybil Pye protested, maintaining that he had written the most beautiful two-stanza poem in the language.

'That's a very sweeping statement' he replied, 'can you support it?'

And Sybil quoted in full:

A slumber did my spirit seal ...

When she reached the end, she looked up at him, still expecting to be challenged. But instead the whole air had altered; he sat silent and absorbed, the serious critic replacing his previous extravagance.

Brooke was human; it would be wrong to depict him otherwise. One teatime at The Orchard two sisters were with him. The elder was supposed to be his current love but another visitor there noticed that he was spending quite a lot of the time flirting with the younger girl and enjoying their combined efforts to attract him. He was constantly searching for fresh excitement, expression, interest.

On 1 June 1910 'Day that I have loved' appeared in the

'Westminster Gazette'. During June he reported Will Crook's lecture to the Fabians in the university 'Review' and in the first week of July went home to attend a Fabian conference. Sidney Webb was one of the speakers and in Rupert's words to Dalton 'old Shaw popped up and down'.

The climax of the academic year came after the term was finished. A party of fifty German students were expected early in August at Cambridge and in their honour the Marlowe Society decided to repeat 'Faustus'.

Before rehearsals for this began, however, the Pye girls, with Rupert and one or two others, sat one evening in a garden where wild briar stocks hung laced together in festoons under the darkly grouped trees. Here they read 'Anthony and Cleopatra' with Rupert playing Anthony. When he came to the great climax and, with a voice scarcely audible, read the soliloquy starting:

I will o'ertake thee, Cleopatra, and
Weep for my pardon, so it must be, for now
All length is torture ...

- the very tree shapes seemed to take on a tragic significance in the summer dusk. Few of them were ever able to read those lines again without hearing his voice.

Brooke's quotable familiarity with Shakespeare was quite extraordinary; the sonnets seemed all there in his head. Lovely lines from them and the plays would be dropped into the air at all sorts of casual moments, and always with such feeling for their true qualities that they remained transfixed in the mind with the background of place and theme which had prompted them.

'Faustus' rehearsals were held in the Pye's house at Grantchester during the second half of July. When the work was over Rupert would read to the Pye girls, the Cornfords and the rest of the company in the sitting room. It was a small and low room, not unlike Rupert's study at King's, with a lamp slung from the ceiling and a narrow door opening straight into the dusk-dark garden. On quiet nights, when watery scents and sounds drifted up from the river, the room almost suggested the cabin of the ship. Brooke sat with his book at a table just below the lamp, the door and the dark sky immediately behind him. The lamplight outlined the proportions of forehead, cheek, chin.

He was entirely English but when he spoke, and especially as now when he read aloud, the clearness of his diction and the expressive freedom in the movement of his lips suggested races whose speech is quicker than ours and whose use of consonants more adroit and telling.

Poems of periods from John Donne onwards he read to them. Short stanzas by Donne and Swinburne, Synge's 'Deirdre' and Meredith's 'Modern Love' made the most impact, the Meredith sonnet-cycle giving him scope for that unforced inflection and variety which so characterised his voice. He would drop from an airy lightness to a sombre, deep emotion with a suddenness and grace that made them catch their breath with wonder.

In spite of this quality of voice and rare power of employing it, he still had no particular talent for acting, so was relegated to the role of Chorus for 'Faustus'. Even in this minor part there was missing at the actual performance in August all the charm of those garden rehearsals, complete with his expressive gestures. With a podgy bull-terrier as the only audience, Rupert stood barefooted under a briar-arch, and appealed with passion to the dog and any chance observer - giving them the joy that the audience would miss.

One day he lay on the floor of the Pye's sitting room playing with another dog, a puppy, who seemed, as he said, able to turn right round inside his skin. The same gay, rapid elasticity marked both their movements, the darting dog and the hands which showed such quick, flexible precision. They were strong and expressive, these hands, with a thumb well divided from the palm. Their shape and articulation imparted a Blake-like quality to his freely direct gestures at rehearsal. For one onlooker, at least, they provoked a strange experience. When Nijinski danced 'The Rose' in London for the first time soon afterwards this friend had the strange feeling of having seen it somewhere before - until the resemblance turned out to be Rupert practising his gestures for the Chorus in 'Faustus'!

When friends thought of Rupert they saw his characteristic pose, full-length on the ground, supported

on one or both elbows. He was sure to adopt this sooner
or later, either on the grass or the floor. An alternative
was to tuck his knees under his chin and clasp his hands
around his calves for support. The full-length posture was
favourite and somehow seemed to be equally suitable for
reading, writing or talking - or all three at once!

Once a strange female was introduced to him at an
inopportune moment while he lay on the floor. He had no
time to change his position so made a gravely courteous
salutation - an actual bow from the floor, which looked
like the height of elegance. The truth was that Brooke
could never appear less than captivating.

> Him, I count him, well-starred.

Matthew Arnold might have written this of his poet
successor from Rugby.

So the night of 'Faustus' came and as the curtain fell
the real exuberance erupted. Term was finished, and
'Faustus' too. Cambridge leapt gaily and weirdly to life
under a fitful harvest moon as the entire company, still in
their costumes of devils, ecclesiastics, virtues and vices,
hired a charabanc and drove in procession through the
sleepy streets to the Cornfords' home in Madingley Road.
Helen of Troy, deserted and desolate at missing the bus,
managed to find a bicycle and sped passionately after the
troupe who leaned out of the conveyance cheering her on!

Safely at Conduit Head, the Cornfords' home, they
danced and drank by the light of torches and a bonfire.
Rupert had been wearing the long-and-full black gown of
Chorus, cut like a medieval scholar's cloak, with a cap the
same sombre colour. These were deemed quite hopeless
for dancing so they had all searched through the stage
props till they found him a close-fitting purple doublet,
dashing to a degree, and long hose in similar style. A
many-pointed gold crown was set on his head and he was
ready for the fray.

Outside the ring of lights, the night had drawn as dark
as the doublet, and his figure melted into it. Then the
spurting gleam from the bonfire would light the points of
the crown, conveying to his head a ghostly detachment!
The lights also caught the golden tone of his hair, escaped

by now from the clutches of the crown and flapping freely as the dance grew wilder. Amid all the bacchanalia, those blazing-bright, intense, merry eyes in a face absorbed yet aware, alert to capture elusive experience.

Beer and cider and sandwiches kept them going long past midnight and the oasis of light flared for a mile or more over the townscape. Finally exhausted, they grabbed up the lowering torches and formed a return procession on foot down the Madingley Road.

The middle of an August night came before everyone reached their beds. A maze of emotion twisted through Rupert's brain as he lay, slightly cider-drunk, recalling eight hectic hours since six that evening. He had kissed one of the girls deliriously in the Cornfords' garden. Now the night was over. They were all dispersed. The torches died down. The moment was past. The kiss was gone. There had been others. There would be more. What did it all mean?

The rest of August, Rupert spent with Dudley Ward touring towns on the South Coast by caravan to promote the Minority Report on the Poor Law. At the end of their route they reached a prearranged camping spot on the far side of the New Forest beside the remote Beaulieu River and slept in tents close to the coast west of the Solent.

Unlike the previous years at Clivedon, Somerset, Noel Olivier was at Beaulieu. She and Rupert lived idyllic days there, walking, embracing under the green cover of branches overhead. They talked of plans for the future. Yet their love did not last. Summer in Hampshire turned to Autumn in Cambridge.

Brooke returned to Rugby for a day or two before starting the fresh term and there he finished 'The Life Beyond', a sonnet on a lost love. It is dated from April to September and ends with the haunting lines:

I thought when love for you died, I should die.
It's dead. Alone, most strangely, I live on.

Rupert was, of course, an inveterate writer of letters and postcards. During the time he knew Noel she received some two hundred epistles from him. These have survived the intervening eighty years of the century.

CHAPTER
6

For his fifth and final year Brooke returned to Cambridge. The Michaelmas term was still a day or two off but he wanted to see how the new Fabian rooms were progressing.

His early period of Youthful Tragedy, as he dubbed it, had passed into perspective and an innate optimism (or anti-pessimism) asserted itself most of the time now. Just before leaving Rugby for Cambridge this time he wrote a long letter to Ben Keeling, mainstay of the Cambridge Fabians, explaining his present attitude to life. The nearest word he could coin was mysticism - not meaning that the whole world was good but rather an absence of despair that it was not. A subtle difference! He saw so much beauty and sudden significance in everyday things that they made his breath stop 'with a gulp of certainty and happiness'.

Hugh Dalton had left last term and began to see much less of Brooke. They had had many memorable times together which neither ever forgot; the wrench of ending the close friendship was less severe than it might have been because it was spread over twelve months. Now it had finally happened it appeared to fall into some sort of perspective. The inevitability of change. Now he almost welcomed change for its own sake, yet still the hankering remained after old faces and friends.

The only Fabian older than Rupert he now dismissed as positively senile, so he felt paternal and almost ancient himself among the current group. They were less cramped in the newly acquired rooms than in Rupert's own and it was in these fresh surroundings on 24 November 1910 that he read them his lecture on 'Democracy and the Arts'. It was brusque and colloquial, with none of his literary grace, yet still extremely effective in its arguments for endowing artists from public funds.

In art as in other fields, Brooke's 'Beardsley etchings' period was a phase of the past now for he had moved over to Rodin, El Greco and Augustus John. In literature his taste and critical faculties were more mature than ever and at the end of 1910, reviewing two volumes of 'The Cambridge History of English Literature', he was merciless in his condemnation of its style:

Dreariness, vagueness and dull dull discomfort settle down on the reader. It is like trying to smell flowers through a blanket. It is amazing that experts and professors of English Literature familiar with so many alive and glowing styles, should write such uniform lustreless English with all the faults of journalese - the flaccidity, the circumlocutions, the trite lifeless unmeaning metaphors, the interminable substantives - without its occasional brightness.

The week before Christmas and the end of the year he spent at Lulworth with the Raverats, where he wrote a light 'Sonnet Reversed' on New Year's Day 1911, while Jacques sketched him idly and dated the drawing - 1.1.11. 'A momentous date' Rupert agreed, 'the start of the Georgian era'.

From Lulworth Brooke began a long Continental tour starting at Munich where Dr Dent had given him numerous introductions. He stayed for three months here, looked after at the pension by Frau Ewald. He liked the Germans but found their culture oppressive and to be resisted at all costs. As the 'Meteor' recorded subsequently at Rugby, he said: 'I have sampled and sought out German culture. It has changed all my views. I am wildly in favour of 19 new Dreadnoughts! German culture must never prevail.'

Despite this outburst he would visit the opera or some other diversion in Munich on most nights. Rupert sat in the opera and let the swirling sounds of Wagner engulf his senses. Then when he had heard enough brass chords he decided to risk 'Rosenkavalier' and Richard Strauss. Into the nights he talked to charming people like a Mr Leuba, so lovingly different from what an unsuccessful journalist would be like in England. He missed most of the brilliance of conversation in the Cambridge manner, arguments with the Raverats, Cornfords, Justin Brooke and Katherine Cox. He visualised Francis and Frances

Cornford; one smoking, the other sitting in her favourite chair on the right of the fire at Conduit Head. And as he sat sipping his milk, Conduit Head automatically reminded him of that night after 'Faustus' the previous August. The cider, the torches, the girl in the garden. England, England. All these blurred images blended into a single searing yearning. He wrote poetry which was improving every month. 'Dead Men's Love' he dated 27 February and 'The Fish' the following month. The latter was intended as a lyric but he turned it into its present 76-line form.

Rupert walked home to the pension in a spring sunset. A German girl was singing folk-songs, accompanying herself on the lute as she sat by a casement window. The jolly Frau Ewald licked her brush as she painted a portrait, one of a regular flow of pictures which the woman produced; she believed in quantity if not imperishable quality. Her son, Paul, called to Rupert in greeting, to chat about his own days at Cambridge. Of the rest, most were English people with a clerical background – not quite in tune with Rupert.

He had enjoyed himself in Munich but finally decided it was time to quit the clatter of the German city where he vowed he ate and slept too much. So he went on to Florence which he had not seen since his Rugby days.

Here he joined his godfather, Robert Whitelaw, and fell once more under the magic mood of Fiesole, its cypresses and spring sun. Originally he had had visions of journeying to Turkey and the mystic Middle East but this was far enough after all. For even as he felt the fresh Italian heat beating down on him through the clear April air, he was thinking of Grantchester again – and of the Old Vicarage where he would be staying from May onwards.

Rupert followed the spring back north across Europe and found its end in the garden at Grantchester. Already he knew the house from previous visits and was attached to it from the day he moved in there.

Where did the magic for Brooke lie in this house? Less with its looks than its character, in a sensitive setting of garden, trees, meadows and stream. The building itself was a wide structure on two main storeys with dormer windows to the attic in the roof above them. Aged brown tiles, ivy groping over mellow rust bricks and a steep gable on the west side all added to its air of antiquity. Inside was a wonder of decrepitude: an elderly stuffed tiger stood fierce guard in black and tan at the top of the stairs, while rooms opened off from one another in an intriguing, inviting way.

Rupert liked immensely the yellow-glass door to an elaborately wrought veranda as it gave the garden a sunny tinge on the dullest day when seen from inside. The scene from the veranda itself was rambling; sweet-smelling shrubs and foliage with, here and there, some relics of the house's eighteenth-century associations such as a sundial sticking out from the dried-up basin of the round pond.

Once-formal flower beds ran wild with neglect and rambler roses twisted unkempt into sweetly strangled arbours. Lichen clothed the outside of the veranda and even that baroque summer house at the far right end of the garden was dilapidated. Yet despite it all, the Old Vicarage was a living place and Brooke much preferred its natural environment to a vapidly formal garden. Once within the picket fence, he felt, a world of past peace breathed gently to life. The afternoon sun shone, throwing shade from the elms on the right further across the lawn, till the old sundial in the centre stood all but engulfed. Not that it would have mattered; time counted for little here.

By now, Rupert was learning to love going into the water as well as on it and he spent hours at various reaches of the river. On Sunday mornings especially, one of his friends used to wake him early to bathe in the dam above Byron's Pool. Time after time on those slumbrous Sunday mornings, with the first haze hardly off the meadows, he would try to dive, invariably failing, hitting the water absolutely flat! Afterwards they would trot back for breakfast, often in the garden of the Old Vicarage, tucking into a meal of eggs followed by bread and butter and honey.

Brooke's bedroom in the Vicarage was littered with books - English, French and German - in wild disorder. After breakfast they might go up there to browse through his collection. In spring, summer and even autumn he always dressed in the same way with an open cricket shirt, flannels and no socks. This garb was at that time regarded as eccentric but Brooke did not care at all, claiming that he could dress on three pounds a year! If the weather was really favourable, he discarded shoes as well as socks to reveal his set of prehensile toes, known to be able to pick up a variety of objects and perform feats arousing envy among his admirers.

He was virtually a vegetarian at Grantchester for he could not eat creatures with whom he felt a kinship. Fish were not included in this category but even so some of his friends wondered whether he was having enough sustenance for his heavy mental and physical exertions.

This sympathy for living creatures kept him busy in the garden where young frogs abounded, the grass being as damp as it was glowing green. Their lives, alleged Rupert, were extremely perilous, for the landlord ate them in secret! So Brooke's long form often appeared at the oddest hours of the day and evening squatting in the long grass, guiding them out of the open and into safer, sheltered paths.

Now that the Grantchester period had really got under way he was shaving more rarely - and badly! Mentally, however, he kept as meticulous as ever and always ready to attack a careless thinker. Despite this Brooke tolerated fools well - even bad poets who must be among the worst of fools.

That same summer of 1911 Helen and Dorothy Houlton, daughters of the local schoolmaster, often went to visit a friend, Kitty Bentley, who was living at the Old Vicarage. Helen and Dorothy stole through the sleeping village very early in the mornings to bathe, throwing small stones up to Kitty's window to awaken her. They called out softly so as not to disturb the other guests but often Brooke appeared at his window and waved gaily to them. If he had been up earlier they met him as he came back from a dip while they were making their way down to the river from the garden.

The girls learned to swim here, where the water was only waist deep, and then when they could manage more safely they found deeper reaches. They chose early morning or late evening for bathing because no-one was about and their mother feared they might shock the local folk! The female form had to be kept religiously hidden. Even their long, voluminous and unbecoming swimming costumes were considered daring.

Several years later they felt that Brooke must have meant them - Dorothy, Kitty and Helen - as they read:

> And when the day is young and sweet,
> Gild gloriously the bare feet
> That run to bathe...
> And there the shadowed waters fresh
> Lean up to embrace the naked flesh.

They hoped he had never seen them in that state, although it was possible. For later on, when they bathed by moonlight in the friendly Granta, they tired of their cumbersome costumes, threw them on the bank with wild shrieks and swam along the dark, deserted river - feeling wicked but free! Brooke wrote:

> They bathe by day, they bathe by night

Virginia Woolf got to know Rupert well that summer of 1911 and stayed at Grantchester. Together they swam quite naked, to their mutual delight at the unconventionality. Virginia spent a week at Grantchester and remembered Rupert as 'consciously and defiantly pagan'. She thought him 'kind and interesting, substantial and good-hearted' but she 'didn't think then much of his poetry, which he read aloud on the lawn'.

Rupert, the Pye girls and one or two others used to bathe by the moon above Byron's Pool. One glorious night, after the exhilaration of swimming in the silver sheen of the river, he clambered up a young poplar to dry himself.

'Be careful, Rupert' one of them warned from below.

'I'm all right thanks - it's wonderful up here.'

At that precise second they all heard his loud unembarrassed laugh as the branch bent right over double under his weight - and he was left hanging wrong way up, with his long hair brushing the grass. In the moonlight they could see his face convulsed with glee at this unaccustomed view of the world.

On the way home that night he told them that he intended to rent a small but useful boathouse near the Old Vicarage. So, true enough, he sought out the owner and arranged the deal. As Rupert investigated it further he found it looked very drear so he decided to decorate the inner walls with a collection of dashing drawings of nudes. No-one would mind, surely? At least he wasn't painting them outside. What could be pleasanter or more artistic? For several days he spent hours at the job and the result revealed him as a talented figure artist. If he had not been absorbed with metre, it might have been murals.

Throughout that summer the boathouse and its decor served its purpose well and his art attracted comment from all the Cambridge circle who saw it. When he finally relinquished the lease to a set of church people the first thing they did was to have those uninhibited, sinful sketches whitewashed into oblivion where they belonged!

To another friend of the times he said: 'Come prepared for bathing and clad in primitive clothes'. The order of each day, he added, was to talk eight hours, read eight hours and sleep eight hours. Exercise took up several hours, not only swimming but walking and cycling. One morning, while he was working on a difficult poem, he plodded on till one o'clock and then *ran* almost all the way to Haslingfield and back before a belated lunch, thinking what should come next. His tall outline diminished to a tiny silhouette jogging along against a frosty sun. The bicycle was coming into its own and still new enough to intrigue Brooke. He used it as a useful way of getting to the university on the increasingly rare days necessary.

Practically every day Brooke was seen somewhere around Grantchester, mainly in the meadows. One evening in late June, the Houlton girls were dawdling homewards when they saw him standing quite still near a tall clump of elms on a little hill called Tartar's Well. He was gazing straight into the sunset, his head thrown high, his fair hair wisping in the wind. Now Tartar's Well has vanished from the local landscape but that image of Brooke endures.

Sometime during that same summer Virginia Woolf and Katherine (Ka) Cox joined Rupert and others at the camp at Clifford Bridge beside the river Teign in south Devon.

When the two girls got there the rest of the party had gone out for the day, 'Leaving nothing for Ka Cox and Virginia to eat on their arrival save a rotting blackberry pudding'. (Quentin Bell on Virginia Woolf). The weather was fine and they enjoyed good music and good conversation around the nightly camp fire. Rupert's circle of friends rippled on outwards. Another companion of the 1911 era was David Garnett, who visited him at Grantchester during the summer term. Then, when holiday time came around again, Garnett and Brooke joined a week's sailing trip on the Norfolk Broads. This time all the Olivier girls came and one or two other young people completed the party - with the inevitable chaperone in the form of Dr Rogers! In those days the Broads were practically deserted. A single sail provided the power for their wherry. When the wind was contrary or dropped altogether they lowered the sail and a patient horse appeared, attached to a tow rope, with a boy sitting sideways on its back.

Life on the Broads was free and peaceful. They swam in the mornings with Rupert still trying to master the craft of diving. Then they lay on deck and talked as the boat slid smoothly through the East Anglian water. Rupert sat forward, propped against the mast, re-writing his thesis on John Webster and the Elizabethan Drama, which had occupied him on and off for most of the year - including his time in Germany, where he had written a number of poems but had done very little research.

They had a sailing dinghy in tow and, if the breeze tempted them, a few went off to sail. Then came the long, golden evenings when the wherry was moored by the bank and the couple of paid hands who navigated it departed to a pub. The days ended with a swim in the darkness and a night-scented kiss on deck. Then with the girls' goodnights ringing in their ears Brooke and Garnett returned to the cabin they shared. For Garnett this was the week of his closest friendship with Brooke, whose immense charm and intelligence he thought were completely unspoilt. In their midnight talks Brooke was simple, sincere and intimate, with a certain lazy warmth. The water lapped at the side of the boat and all was well with their world: the new Georgian world of 1911.

CHAPTER

7

Brooke's poetry of this period could hardly have been less like that by Frances Cornford who believed - according to Rupert - that poetry should be short, simple, naive. Yet despite their different styles they were good friends and candid critics of each other's work.

For some months now they had nursed hopes of bringing out volumes of their poems but so far nothing had materialised. Brooke told her how the reviewers would mistake their respective sexes, as so often happened, and say that Mr Cornford had some pretty thoughts but Miss Brooke was always intolerable! Or else they could be called Major Cornford and the Widow Brooke.

Now, in September 1911, Brooke finally found a publisher who was interested in handling a volume of his verse. The man with the vision to encourage Brooke was Frank Sidgwick, of Sidgwick and Jackson, who had also been at Rugby. He had already read random poems by Brooke in one or two of the literary periodicals when Rupert brought him the first collection of poems. So Sidgwick already knew, before reading the complete manuscript, that Brooke could write with extreme beauty and could run with a savage joy to more provocative verse.

At this initial meeting with Brooke, Sidgwick was surprised and pleased to discern that he had none of the ordinary illusions of young poets. The publisher accepted the volume in principle but asked to see Brooke again to discuss exactly which poems should appear. At this next meeting Brooke told Sidgwick that he was eager not to overbalance the book in the direction of unimportant prettiness and so defended the inclusion of certain poems which Sidgwick queried on the grounds of suitability. 'Well', Brooke persevered, 'people need not read the parts which are new and serious, or they think objectionable. You know, I occasionally feel, like Ophelia, that I've turned "thought and affliction, passion, hell itself...to favour and to prettiness.'"

Sidgwick respected his wishes and risked the inclusion of some 'unpleasant' or 'provocative' poems. One of Brooke's continual struggles was to avoid the mere prettiness in poetry and aim higher - and deeper. It was an immense effort for him to achieve the satisfactory expression he told Sidgwick.

In the 'immeasurably autumnal' air pervading Grantchester, Brooke continued his consciously pagan existence. His feet still bare; his bed often in the open; disdaining tobacco and meat. A complicated compound of vigour and sensitivity. However 'sunburnt and slapdash' - as a contemporary described him and his literature - they were both intensely, vitally alive.

He worked hard at his poetry all the time. Proofs of his book fluttered on leaf-strewn grass, while poems lay about all over the place with spaces for an unfinished phrase or line. One day during 1911, for instance, he was completing 'Town and Country' when he reached the penultimate verse. Squatting in the garden at Grantchester he asked his friends who were there what was the highest thing in nature. Then he glanced around, decided it was a leaf in the sun and completed the first two lines of that verse, which had borne a blank space till then:

Unconscious and unpassionate and still,
Cloud-like we lean and stare as bright leaves stare

That first volume of poems was typeset and printed in the sedate Victorian building of Billings, just outside Guildford Railway station, and even the compositors expressed excitement at some of its lines as they handled the type and pulled proofs of it - certainly an unusual occurrence.

Meanwhile, up at Grantchester, at the same time as passing the proofs, he was 'wallowing in Webster'. As the autumn wore on he was finding it increasingly essential to be near the British Museum to gather the final facts for his thesis. Yet however hospitable Eddie Marsh invariably was, he felt he could not stay there for a long period so for the next six or seven weeks he found some dreary rooms in Charlotte Street, their only advantage being the proximity to the museum.

Here he suffered from the sudden contrast between his healthy Grantchester life and the late autumn mists of the metropolis. He worked far too hard all day on Webster without troubling much about food and afterwards he went round to Marsh's flat in Gray's Inn or to other friends in the artistic area. Several times he tottered across the lawns of Gray's Inn barely able to reach the gaunt, deep-buff building. This pace could not be kept up for long, it was clear. Always he had that tendency towards sickness - apparent after using up too much nervous energy - although he had not been really ill yet.

London life became too much for him by the middle of November so as soon as he had got his material from the Museum he told Marsh he would not stay any longer but would write the final draft back at Grantchester. This had to be finished by Christmas and actually took the latter half of November and earlier part of December, when the Old Vicarage was a 'House of Usher' matching his mood of gloom and fatigue.

How strange, he thought, the dramatic difference between summer and winter at the same place: from sun and splendour to dank despair. He looked out past the veranda but saw only a stark tracery of trees, black-branched, their lives in suspense; the grass no longer grew; the river looked muddy, morose; and a grey fog-shroud settled over it all. He was worn out.

Near the end of this time his younger brother visited Grantchester and found that Rupert had hardly been to bed for a week, trying to complete his thesis.

'You must ease up, Rupert, you know, or you'll have a breakdown. No blessed thesis is worth that.'

Rupert nodded but was compelled to go on till he had finished it. As he scrawled the last line he sank back in a chair exhausted and lay there for several hours. He was too tired to rest, he had gone too far. He felt he must get away from it all again so packed a case quickly and delivered the thesis to Cambridge. Then he caught the late train back to London to see Marsh again. Gradually restlessness was growing within him which could not be satisfied, stifled; an urge to be elsewhere and then a nostalgia for where he had been. An eternal buffeting between past and present, here and there. In London, he soon realised how ill he was and hurried home to the sanctuary of Bilton Road a week before Christmas.

By now 'Poems, 1911' were published, although he was past caring about their reception, for at the best of times he lost interest in anything as soon as he had created it. He could not claim complete indifference, however, for he had fought hard for the retention of those 'objectionable' poems.

'Lust' was one of those he succeeded in keeping, although he compromised - in a letter dated 20 September - on a modified title of 'Libido'. Despite this Brooke regretted his weakness, for whenever he came across a copy of the book he struck out 'Libido' with a definite, defiant line and wrote 'Lust' in large capitals! In the copy he inscribed for Francis and Frances Cornford, later acquired by the collector John Schroder, this alteration has been made. Brooke has also changed 'greasy' to 'queasy' in the poem 'Jealousy'.

The line now reads:

Senility's queasy furtive love-making

The reviews reached Brooke at Rugby and on the whole could be called most encouraging, although the half-dozen allegedly unpleasant poems received critical comment and attention out of all proportion to their quantity in the total of fifty.

'The Spectator' applauded the poems wholeheartedly, commenting that 'unlike most youthful work, it shows a curious absence of imitation and a strenuous originality ... a book of rare and remarkable promise.' 'The Saturday Review', remarking rather obscurely, told him to 'mar no more trees with writing love-songs in their barks.' Edward Thomas in the 'Daily Chronicle' forecast that Brooke would be a poet and not a little one, going on in exhortation: 'Copies should be bought by every one over forty who has never been under forty. It will be a revelation.'

Quite a few exceptions were taken to the 'unpleasant' poems, which were too realistic for 1911, one reviewer calling it 'a volume of *blague*'. Public feeling, like that of Rupert's friends, could be summed up in Arthur Benson's view of the poems 'some very charming, some strangely ugly'. The notice which meant the most to Brooke was by Eddie Marsh in the 'Poetry Review': 'A too conscientious critic might argue that he is not sincere, that he rides round the world as though it were a circus, crashing through the emotions as if through paper hoops...Meanwhile let us be thankful for a man who can make so much beauty.'

Although Brooke still felt very tired over Christmas he was determined to keep an arrangement, made a long time before, to meet Cambridge friends at a fortnight's reading party down in Lulworth, starting from the last few days of the year.

He managed to get there but almost on arrival had the nervous collapse which had been threatening since the autumn. The final cause of the collapse was Ka Cox. Rupert felt close to both Noel Olivier and Ka but the episode at Lulworth seems to have precipitated stronger feelings for Ka. She and Lytton Strachey formed two of the reading party, while the painter Henry Lamb arrived two or three days later. Lamb started flirting with Ka, much to Rupert's fury. He became even more livid when she told him that she felt attracted to Lamb - the upshot being Rupert's near-breakdown.

All he could do was to stay in bed, with hardly any food or sleep, until he could get back to his doctor who saw at once that he had lost a lot of weight and diagnosed 'a seriously introspective condition'. 'You need an utter change from all this' the doctor decided. 'Your mother is staying in Cannes so I advise you to go over and join her there. Just the thing for you at present.'

Rupert acquiesced and made his weary way to the South of France, where the stuffy, upper-class atmosphere immediately grated on him. He was determined to leave as soon as he could decently do so, and making his excuses to the completely uncomprehending Mrs Brooke, he went on to the more congenial and familiar pension at Munich.

The cure here for his previous lack of food and sleep seemed to be overeating and oversleeping, coupled with complete absence of exercise and thought. Brooke had to force himself into this state of mental stagnation so alien to his normal nature. It was a real effort to relax.

A letter from Eddie Marsh, then on Admiralty duties in Portsmouth, cheered him early in February for it enclosed the notice of his poems, which Marsh was proposing for 'Poetry Review'. Marsh mentioned how 'Dead Men's Love' offended many people. Brooke could never understand these objections.

> Hands out, they hurried, knee to knee

- this was the type of line which offended pre-war readers, still not free from starchy Victorian hypocrisy.

Rupert rose late at the pension, lived off milk and stout - separately - and generally did as he was told by the capable, capacious Frau Ewald.

The secret and surprising thing was that, unknown to Mrs Brooke, Rupert and Ka had arranged to meet on the Continent. They went on to Munich from a Verona rendezvous. Ka looked after him as a lover and, as he gained strength, she broke it to him that she had still been meeting Henry Lamb. Rupert felt appalled that Ka could divide her feelings in this way. Towards the end of February they returned home. Rupert wrote nothing at that time, except his letters.

Despite this dramatic phase in their relationship, Rupert remained close to Ka. By the time he managed to reverse her feelings the following year he no longer really loved her. The irony of life. Yet when he left half a dozen letters written in case of his death, the one to Ka ended: 'You were the best thing I found in life. If I have memory, I shall remember. You know what I want for you. I hope you will be happy, marry and have children. It is a good thing I die. Good-bye child. Rupert.'

This constant inconstancy of hearts worried him sometimes. There did not seem to be sense in it. He wanted love to last always but it never did. So he drifted from one girl to another. Searching for something. Through the years this is what his life became, a search, an endless quest - for what? Brooke did not know, could not tell. Life, love, their power, their meaning, their lack of meaning. So he went on searching. Judging by a letter to Ka in March 1912, soon after he got back to England, they still seemed to be on good terms.

The same year, after a walk in springtime Sussex trying to trace the home of Henry James, he and a friend reached Rye. Here Rupert sat down in the medieval Mermaid Club and wrote to her lightheartedly, recounting their adventures across the middle of Sussex. When he had finished he strolled out in the afternoon air of the old town. The teashops with the little Tudor windows were starting to serve; the church stood reminding him of the one at Grantchester; and at four o'clock stillness descended on the timbered facades of that little world within a world which has been Rye for four centuries or more. Nothing stirred, though a new-fangled motor car struck an incongruous note. Rupert lingered in Rye for a day or two, remembering Ka. This was a place of love: the rooftops of Rye set high on a hill. Because he had loved Ka, he wrote flippantly. That familiar opposite vein reacting against his feelings.

Meanwhile in March or April he wrote two poems, each reflecting - in the season of spring - the emotions of fading love. The haunting 'Beauty and Beauty' with its misty ecstasies 'eddying, dizzying, closing round.' And then in its second stanza:

> Where Beauty and Beauty met,
> Earth's still a-tremble there,
> And winds are scented yet,
> And memory-soft the air,
> Bosoming, folding glints of light,
> And shreds of shadowy laughter;
> Not the tears that fill the years
> After - after -

And after came the 'Song' with its sadness of that spring:
> All suddenly the wind comes soft,
> And Spring is here again;
> And the hawthorn quickens with buds of green,
> And my heart with buds of pain.

One or two recent writers have placed undue emphasis on a single homosexual encounter between Brooke and a friend while at Cambridge. Rupert himself described this in a characteristicaly natural letter soon afterwards. Perhaps it would be more accurate to ascribe any neurosis he might have suffered to the fact that English girls did not normally consummate a love affair at that period. Perhaps inhibiting to someone as intense as Rupert. Certainly homosexuality as a way of life repelled him and, as Timothy Rogers has pointed out, Rupert cut Lytton Strachey dead, in public, in the foyer at Drury Lane.

Eddie Marsh went up to Rugby to stay for a few days with Rupert, who had added a bout of 'flu to the nervous illness. There they walked along the Avon's banks, as Brooke did when a boy. He felt better after this and cheered up still more with the arrival of Geoffrey Keynes for an evening meal.

Gradually Rupert was recovering. At Easter, he was advised to have another change of scene, so he went down to Lyndhurst, where he stayed at a house called Beach Shade, a name he was quick to see symbolised his current state of mind. For here in the heart of the ancient New Forest, he wrote to Hugh Dalton of his troubles and travels:

Dear Hugh,
You were good to me. It doesn't matter about the scientist who got a fellowship for two reasons
(1) Nothing matters (2) They will give me a fellowship next year. The electors seem agreed on that.

The scientist, you see, had no more shots. I have one more. Both our dissertations were extremely good. He discovered a very important thing about the blood of coal miners. It needs far less oxygen than you think. And it follows they can live for longer and far oftener when the worst happens, than you suppose.

Friend of my laughing, careless youth, where are those golden hours now? Where now the shrill mirth of our burgeoning intellects? And by what dubious and deleterious ways am I come down to this place of shadows and eyeless pain? In truth, I have been for some months in Hell. I have been very ill. I am very ill. In all probability I shall be very ill. It is thought by those that know me best (viz. myself) that I shall die. Nor do I greatly want to live, the savour of life having oddly left it, and my mind being worn and flabby, a tenth of anything it used to be.

I do nothing. I eat and sleep and rest. My thoughts buzz drearily in a vacuum. I went in January to a slightly American nerve-specialist who said I was deplorably unwell. He made me drink stout and swallow the compressed blood of bullocks. In consequence I am now enormously fat. Boys laugh at me in the street. But that is partly, also, on account of my manner. For I am more than a little gone in my head, since my collapse.

I go back to Germany soon. They are a slow race and will not know I am stupid. I shall never appear in England again. I shall never write poetry or limpid prose again. I may ultimately become a sub-reader of English Philology in the John Hopkins University, Wa. (or Ma. or Ra....). I am a despicable, toothless creature and I mock at the Spring. I salute you from these depths.

Give my love to the Middle Temple.

> *Ever,*
> *Rupert*

Lulworth, Cannes, Munich, Lyndhurst with its New Forest memories of Noel. And now back to Germany again. This time, however, he went for a return visit to Berlin where he spent most of the time with Dudley Ward and his wife.

The spring had really reached England by the mellow and magic early days of May. In Berlin, Brooke sat at a table of the Café des Westens. He looked around him at the sweating Germans and then up at the humid, cloud-strewn sky. A throbbing wave of loneliness, longing, clutched him - and he scrawled down:

> Just now the lilac is in bloom,
> All before my little room;

No more need be said. The clatter of the café faded from his ears; the smell of sweat changed magically to poppy and pansy; his eyes saw beyond the gilt furniture and the urgent city, to the sights of springtime in Grantchester - cool, clean and clear - and the sense-swirling, intoxicating, simple splendour of it. He ached for England with a sincere, searing pain. The only way to stop it was to convey his emotions. In a few days he had completed one hundred and forty lines of 'this hurried stuff' as he called it when sending it on to Eddie Marsh.

Here, for the first time, he perfected that mature marriage of light and lyric; wit and wonder. 'The Old Vicarage, Grantchester' has come to be recognised as one of the most memorably evocative landscapes in all literature. No-one reading it has failed to be transported deep into the greenery of Grantchester at that supreme moment of spring.

The poem did not have to wait long for publication. Only a month after Marsh had received it and realised its worth, it appeared in the June 1912 'Basileon' under the title of 'Fragments from a poem to be entitled "The Sentimental Exile"'.

Before leaving Berlin in the sticky summer heat he worked for a month on a one-act play which turned out to be the melodrama 'Lithuania', his only work for the stage.

The play is based on the idea of a son, long since left home, returning with a fortune to his poor peasant family who kill him for the money before discovering who he is. John Drinkwater acknowledged that though homespun and, almost threadbare in texture it had a beauty that none but a poet could have achieved. Drinkwater and Brooke were to meet later in the year.

Rupert returned from Berlin in June, happier, heavier and healthier. One day in September it occurred to Marsh and Brooke that there should be scope for a book of collected poems by a dozen or so of the younger poets, an idea which before long blossomed into the anthology of 'Georgian Poetry, 1911-12'. Marsh gathered some prospective contributors together to hear of this proposal and then they all went along to visit the home-to-be of the 'Poetry Review' at 35 Devonshire Street, Bloomsbury.

That first occasion when Drinkwater met Brooke there were only a few moments they could talk together, yet even there he got the impression of an extraordinarily alert intelligence, finely equipped with both wit and penetrative power. Drinkwater realised that no-one of Brooke's years could ever have had in greater measure the gifts that could be used to make easily swayed admiration gape: and no man was ever more wholly indifferent to any such conquests. Drinkwater found humour in abundance but of witty insincerity, no trace. Never was a personality more finely balanced. He was properly glad of his qualities; also, he was properly careless of them.

This meeting between Brooke and Drinkwater was on 20 September when they lunched at Marsh's home in Raymond Buildings by Gray's Inn. Among the other guests were Wilfrid Gibson, Harold Munro, and Arundel de Re, associate editor of 'Poetry Review'. It was also Brooke's first meeting with Gibson. After the exciting seeds were sown for the Georgian poetry book, the day ended with Marsh's putting Rupert, Gibson and their musician friend Denis Browne up for the night.

Eddie Marsh was performing his self-imposed task of patronage well although there were some who remained convinced that beneath all his efforts lay a certain snobbery and an inclination for reflected glory. Whatever the truth, Rupert did meet several of his brighter contemporaries through the medium of Marsh: Walter de la Mare, John Masefield, John Galsworthy together with the legendary figures of Katherine Mansfield and John Middleton Murry.

Brooke accepted an invitation to visit Katherine and John at their home in the country. Rupert Brooke, the debonair, Murry called him. Brooke told them, with a happy laugh, macabre and horrifying tales of old women in lovely houses being devoured by their own cats, and of strange and sinister happenings among the Lithuanian peasants. This was the play, of course.

One early autumn evening Brooke, Frederick Goodyear, Katherine Mansfield and Murry tramped miles over the salt marshes in the dusk from Runcton Cottage, singing the choruses of Goodyear's innumerable songs. A queer quartet vanishing into the gloom as their voices wafted away into the night. Then after the rustic interlude Rupert returned to the life of London and Georgian Poetry.

CHAPTER 8

Exactly three weeks after the luncheon launching the first book of Georgian poetry, Eddie Marsh had gathered and prepared enough examples of the major young poets to compose a representative volume. The next day he sent them to the printer to be set. In just over two months the book appeared. Before this Rupert went to stay with the Wards in Berlin again from where, during November, he sent frequent communications concerning techniques for marketing the book successfully.

From Berlin he kept in touch too with Hugh Dalton. Their friendship had now survived for six years, across the whole three years of King's and another three from the distances of Grantchester - London - Europe.

Dear Hugh,
I am, as you say, dead. Further processes even have set in.

> *Though one be mild as Moses,*
> *His meekness clouds and closes;*
> *In the end he decomposes;*
> *And he is sure to smell.*

As Swinburne, or you, or someone of the Romantics put it.
I am on pretext of doing a dissertation here. Actually I
have not done a word. I spend my time in making love to
female dancers. They pirouette scornfully away ... After
the 10th December I shall come to London. Then I shall
sit one night and repeat poetry to you, and you will repeat
dirty stories to me; till 8.30 a.m. Then I shall go to bed.
In January I go to America for three years. Cambridge
must be full of people one knows. Perhaps it is nicer not
to be there. But I am sorry not to see them capering in
the Greek Play. I have discovered the real division of
mankind into the Petrine and the Jesuine; those who are
crucified head downwards and those who are crucified

Previous page: At work in the garden of the Old Vicarage, Grantchester, 1910. From the author's collection.

Rupert Brooke's grave in the island of Scyros in the Aegean. From the author's collection.

right way up. It is immensely important. Perhaps the
greatest discovery of the Twentieth Century. Beyond that
I have done nothing; written but one line, but that a good
one. Ah, love, there is no something in the sun!
It ends a sonnet (- but what sonnet?) It is the truest line
in English except Meredith's 'And Life, some say, is
worthy of the Mews.' Be in London in December.

Rupert.

Heart, you are a restless paper scrap.

The line above was from 'The Unfortunate', one of six
poems published under his name in the 'Poetry Review'
during his sojourn in Berlin. Another piece appearing
while he was away came out in the 'Cambridge Magazine'.
In it Rupert reviewed the Post-Impressionist Exhibition of
Art seen at the Grafton Galleries that autumn. He paid his
last of several visits there on 5 November, just before
leaving for Berlin.

Brooke preferred the name Expressionism to Post-
Impressionism and although he loved the genuine Post-
Impressionists, he maintained that some of the pictures
should have been in the Royal Academy, some in the New
English Art Club and a few in the muck-heap!

Twenty works of Matisse conveyed to Brooke a world
'clean, lovely and inhuman as a douche of cold water.'
Picasso he considered very different and distinctly inferior
and thought that the artist did not care about colour.
Picasso's two best drawings he found 'lovely and self-
sufficient and inexplicable as a fugue'.

Brooke could not praise the English school much,
although approving of the 17-year-old Stanley Spencer's
'John Donne arriving in Heaven' perhaps partly as the
subject interested Brooke. He decided also that Wyndham
Lewis resembled Picasso in method; that Roger Fry knew
what a good picture was; and Mr Gill was one of the three
or four great sculptors of the past hundred years.

Back from Berlin Rupert branched out again into fresh
interests. His first action on arrival in December was to
ask Eddie Marsh if a meeting could be arranged with the
Irish actress Cathleen Nesbitt whom Brooke had admired in

a play during a hectic summer's theatre-going and remembered ever since. At the time Rupert requested this meeting Cathleen was playing Perdita in 'A Winter's Tale' at the Savoy Theatre. He had actually attended the first night.

Marsh managed this in a remarkably diplomatic manner, well worthy of his political affiliations. Within forty-eight hours of Rupert's request Marsh met Cathleen in Henry Ainley's dining room at the Savoy. By coincidence Miss Nesbitt also expressed to Marsh a wish to meet someone - Gilbert Cannan - so Eddie had a ready-made opportunity for organising a supper at Raymond's Buildings a week later. Its apparent purpose was to effect the meeting between Cathleen and Cannan but, quite by casual chance, Rupert Brooke was invited too! Eddie told Rupert of the plan and the two of them slapped each other's backs at the way it had all been arranged.

Cathleen and Rupert found an immediate fusion of interests and sympathies. There was the obvious link of the love of the theatre; they were young and highly intelligent; and both deeply devoted to poetry. Rupert fell in love with her.

'I adore you' he wrote in these and many other words. They met whenever the chance came but both led busy lives that winter. She loved him too but not enough to want to marry him. Nevertheless, isolated, idyllic days lit their next five months.

Rupert was back at his brilliant best and around Christmas developed a passion for the Hippodrome revue 'Hullo, Ragtime!' He went to see it ten times altogether. Once was on New Year's Eve. After the performance, he and Marsh and some others walked down through the deserted Long Acre and Covent Garden. They passed Floral Street and the gallery entrance to the Royal Opera House which they knew so well, then came down to the Strand and Fleet Street and finally on to the steps of St. Paul's, where they saw in the New Year of 1913. The bells boomed out at midnight and the crowd sang 'Auld Lang Syne'.

As they eventually dispersed Rupert's party strolled the streets around Holborn, passing the row of Tudor fronts there and at long last winding a way to Raymond Buildings and the legal peace of Gray's Inn. The clock chimed three before the night was over. The inn was still gaslit, and the vestiges lingered of the old days but now they were on the brink of a brave new world - halfway between both. Nowhere, quite, at this moment. The old year had gone, the new one come. Perhaps all was change all the time. Still so many questions and no absolute answers. Rupert went to sleep with the safe three sides of the inn buildings sheltering him from the past and present until next day.

One of his friends of this era was St John Ervine, later the distinguished writer and playwright, but at that time a young dramatic critic. Here is his impression of Brooke, written exclusively for this book, and in his unique way:

My memories of Rupert Brooke are few. He was still an undergraduate at Cambridge when we met for the first time, and I cannot recall just what it was that brought about our meeting. Anyhow, we became friends and, in the short time that was left to him, we saw much of him. We lived then in a charming flat on the Finchley Road, on the verge, so to speak, of the Hampstead Garden Suburb, which was a great novelty then, a daring and most attractive attempt at town planning. This flat was a meeting place for young people like ourselves, who were mostly young Fabians, as Rupert was, and very eager to put the world to rights.

When Brooke came down, he lived for a while in Gray's Inn, and it was here that he met Cathleen Nesbitt, a young and very intelligent actress, who was, perhaps, too intelligent to become a celebrated player, though she became well known not only as a very capable but an absolutely trustworthy actress, who did her job well. Whether she and Rupert were ever formally engaged to be married, I don't know for certain, but there was a general impression that they were more or less engaged. Just what Rupert meant to do in London, apart from writing poetry, I don't know. He never talked of any other work that he wished to do, and he was, we thought, tolerably well off, so he could, of course, please himself about that. Anyhow, I never heard him talk about a possible profession, and my general impression is that he meant to be a poet and only a poet.

I need not tell you what an impression Rupert made on all who saw him. The word beautiful is not one which anybody nowadays likes to apply to a man, but it is the only word that is applicable to Brooke. I remember a night, when, returning to my flat from Fleet Street after a first night in the theatre, I was feeling fagged and out of sorts with my fellow men who lay sprawling in an ungainly heap on the seats in the Golders Green tube train. Suddenly, at Leicester Square I think (probably from the Hippodrome), the door opened and in stepped Rupert, as resplendent as a Greek god. I can't begin to tell you what his effect was. The whole carriage full of tired and sprawling and desperately dingy people lit up as if he were the sun god himself and had set fire to them.

He was an extraordinarily handsome man, very masculine in every respect, as I knew him, and with nothing in the least niminy-piminy about him. He was a male man. There is, I believe, a tendency among those who did not know him and never even saw him to think that he was effeminate. I assure you he wasn't - not in my knowledge, nor did I ever hear anybody who knew him suggest that he was. He was a tall, robust-looking man, with broad shoulders, and he looked as if he were physically strong. His hair was golden - and I mean golden. I don't mean yellow. It looked like gold, and it shone like gold. His complexion was healthy and his eyes were bright. He was, I repeat, essentially male. How strong physically he was I do not know, but I should hate to have been his opponent in a scrap. He could, I feel, have done a good deal of damage. Such a man, one would have expected to be vain. But Rupert had no vanity that an able undergraduate ought not to have.

He was modest and unassuming, and he did not attempt to monopolise the conversation. He was not, indeed, a good talker, and could sit in company without opening his mouth. I had nearly said he was as silent as John Millington Synge, but nobody could possibly have been as silent as he was reputed to be. As a sparkling conversationalist, then, Rupert simply did not exist. He was a young man of amazing good looks, godlike good looks, who seemed certain to be a good and perhaps even a great poet. It will not surprise me if I am told that he played games well. The 'precious' legend is entirely false. He could, of course, do his bit of posing, like the rest of us, and take up eccentric attitudes, such as we have all at sometime assumed, but he was not conspicuously posturing or eccentric, and if he was aware of his extraordinarily handsome appearance, he never said or did anything to show that he was.

I fear that I may be making him seem a little commonplace, but that is not what I wish to do. He was exceptional in several ways, but he did not make a profession of being exceptional. I have met people with half his talent who did far more showing off in an hour than he did in the whole of my acquaintance with him. His most charming characteristic was his likeability. I suppose he had some enemies - who that has character hasn't? - but I was fortunate enough not to meet them. I'm sure I should have thought them detestable if I had! He didn't like London. 'The dreadful state of busied indolence London reduces me to, stops me from ever carrying out any intent, or doing anything' he wrote to my wife in an undated letter, 'I have done no work in the last fortnight...' On a postcard - he was addicted to postcards - he writes 'I'm sorry to be so incompetent. London life is too much for me.' On another, he says 'There is a nightmare of a fog which makes me feel ill. I hate London!'

One evening in January, St. John Ervine dined with Rupert, Cathleen and Marsh and then the three men went on to one of the classic Shaw-Belloc debates. Later still, back at Raymond Buildings, Rupert read his completed 'Lithuania' to them.

When Cathleen Nesbitt and Rupert first met she was still getting over a very recent relationship with actor Henry Ainley while Rupert was recovering from the Ka Cox affair. Rupert called Cathleen 'incredibly, inordinately. devastatingly, immortally, calamitously, hearteningly, adorably beautiful'.

They saw the 'Hello Ragtime' revue half a dozen times together. At this period Rupert had been lent a flat in Thurloe Square. One Sunday when she visited him there she had a toothache and he tucked her up on the sofa with

an aspirin washed down with hot milk. They knew they
were in love. 'I adore you', Rupert wrote to her. The
four months to April 1913 were blurred into a 'colourful
kaleidoscope' as Cathleen put it.

They often used to take a train into the country and go
for long walks holding hands. They would make these
trips on Sundays and Mondays. If they spent the night at
an inn they occupied separate rooms. Rupert sat on her
bed and they talked into the small hours – but they did not
become lovers. Nor did they live in an 'exalted
atmosphere' perpetually but Rupert's spirits inspired
Cathleen 'with a kind of vitality and gaiety which was not
really in my nature' as she expressed it in her
autobiography.

So the whirl went round and round. Rupert and
Geoffrey Keynes saw Cathleen Nesbitt acting in 'General
John Regan'. Brooke met many of the most promising
people of the day: D. H. Lawrence, Granville-Barker,
Rose Macaulay, James Barrie, Robert Bridges and the
Georgian poets. Through Eddie Marsh he also got to know
the Asquiths, George Wyndham and the Bernard Shaws.

Eddie Marsh observed a gradual change in Brooke's
outlook, perhaps dating from the late Grantchester period
and accentuated after his illness of 1912: a shift he
described as Brooke's discovery that goodness was the most
important thing in life – 'that immortal beauty and
goodness' as Rupert wrote later.

Brooke still felt the urge to get right away from the
London and even the English scene but he went on
enjoying himself for the first few months of the year. He
had an insatiable appetite for shows and plays and he
visited the Russian Ballet whenever they came. It was the
gallery or pit for these expeditions as, although he had a
private allowance, it was not enough for extravagance.

He indulged in this last London fling as he knew that
sooner or later he would be off to America and possibly
beyond. This was the sort of life one could only lead for
a limited time. Everything happened at such an endless,
remorseless pace that he would crack eventually. Yet,
although he pleaded that it left no time for serious study
or composition, several poems emerged from this pre-
travel period of early 1913.

Elated at having won a £30 prize offered by 'Poetry Review' for the best poem of 1912 in that publication, he and Cathleen celebrated suitably with some other friends. Elated, yes; but not conceited for he felt several others were better than his own.

By now new poems and prose had been accepted by various journals as well as his regulars. 'The Night Journey', for instance, in 'Rhythm', with its imaginative impressions of a train leaving a station and all the mingled emotions it aroused. Rupert was always travelling in a train of thought, forever aiming at elusive lands: happy, restless, wondering. The constant search for the perfect place, for ecstasy. He wrote in a line from an unpublished sonnet:

Love soars from earth to ecstasies unwist

Then back to earth again to an imaginary Cambridgeshire folk-song invented by Brooke while staying with Jacques and Gwen Raverat at the village of Croydon-cum-Clopton. Clopton does not now exist, he explained, the inhabitants having been wiped out by the Black Death. How did it come to be told to Rupert? Allegedly by his taking it down from the Clopton blacksmith. So there was still a lot of boyish nonsense in Brooke, now aged 25. Before his next birthday he told friends he would not now marry as he was too old.

On 8 March he was finally awarded his Fellowship at Cambridge but overlooked the actual date and had to send a telegram of apology for absence. Next week, however, he remembered to go there to be admitted or 'churched' as he termed it. Then the following day he caught the 4.55 p.m. train back to London again. Many times he had travelled on this train in his undergraduate and later days, as it reached London in time for the evening shows or dinner. He saw it as an old, trusted friend that stayed the same in a shifting world - and got him to Town by around seven o'clock!

The Fellowship thesis on John Webster was subsequently reviewed as showing 'a scholarship remarkable in one so young'. Brooke received many messages congratulating him on the honour which he did not take at all seriously. One of these came from John Masefield at Well Walk. Masefield also mentioned that Granville-Barker was very interested in Brooke's play and urged him to continue writing drama.

Rupert used to devote almost all day to meeting his various London friends at this time, which necessitated sending a steady stream of postcards all over the place to organize these arrangements. He augmented his correspondence by the still-novel telephone, invaluable with the intricate timing often involved. These surviving scraps of day-to-day notes make a poignant impact on an observer.

Just about March, he wrote his sonnet 'Love', starting:

Love is a breach in the walls, a broken gate ...

On the back of the rough manuscript is written, in Brooke's hasty hand, two notes to remind him of these routine rendezvous. One reads simply '49 Bedford Square at 11.30' and the other 'T.S.M. Well Walk Tuesday'. The latter was presumably Thomas Sturge Moore. How tragically trivial these jottings seem, buried on the back of a library manuscript, yet they are as real and alive as his poems and letters: evidence of the life he led, knowledge that he was in certain places at actual times. The little human touches, too. In his sad 'Song', for instance, with its verse:

Love came our quiet way
Lit pride in us, and died in us,
All in a winter's day.
There is no more to say.

Rupert's original pale pencil handwriting bears a semicolon after 'lit pride in us' and not a comma.

More arrangements - this time Brooke and Drinkwater were to visit a theatre but, as Rupert was invited as the guest, he wrote urgently asking how he should be dressed. Normally he would have worn his Norfolk jacket and flannels but he did not want to embarrass Drinkwater. He was very relieved to learn that anything would be acceptable - and evening dress was not necessary! After the play they stayed up most of the night talking poetry, the Georgian venture, literature and life in general.

'Georgian Poetry 1911-12' included five of Brooke's best poems from this period: 'The Old Vicarage, Grantchester'; 'Dust'; 'The Fish'; 'Town and Country'; 'Dining Room Tea'. They had a lot to discuss for the first edition sold out virtually on the date of publication, so that a second printing had been ordered. The prime minister was one of the first purchasers.

Maurice Hewlett told Eddie Marsh that Brooke was truly a poet, regarding Rupert, W. H. Davies and Walter de la Mare as the best three in the book. Others were to be hardly less noted; Masefield, Alfred Noyes, Newbolt, James Elroy Flecker, Wilfrid Gibson, Sturge Moore. Quite a constellation. A new movement had been born, given expression. Alert, alive, anti-Victorian, anti-Edwardian, pro-Georgian. Essentially of the twentieth century and forward looking, seeking fresh forms.

His trip grew nearer, although the financial hurdle was not quite topped, as he could only rake together about £200. Meanwhile he kept up his contributions to periodicals. For 'Poetry and Drama' he wrote on the poems of John Donne. And to the 'Blue Review' he sent two poems, 'Love' and 'The Busy Heart' with its opening line:

Now that we've done our best and worst, and parted

A final article written before leaving revealed that, in his opinion, 'Appius and Virginia' attributed to John Webster was not actually his work. Brooke had twenty copies of this reprinted and several survive.

Spring reached London too, as the trees of Gray's Inn coloured the drab brick facades and daisies dotted its lawns with white. Rupert had moved to South Kensington but was still in the thick of the social whirl. At last the chance came for his travels to turn into reality, chief credit for this being due to Naomi Royde-Smith. For several years she had been an admirer of Brooke's verse and she was delighted to see some of it published in the 'Westminster Gazette', where she worked.

In 1912 she graduated to the literary editorship of the

weekly and met Rupert for the first time. She became fond of him at once and when she discovered he wanted a drastic change of scene - preferably in the New World - she managed to persuade her editor to commission a series of articles on America and Canada from first-hand experience. Rupert was more than ready for such an opportunity,which meant that he didn't need to worry about financing the trip. By then he had wearied of London's endless activity in a circle revolving to no visible effect. It had all become a bit too precious for Rupert who never aspired to society for its own social sake.

He jumped at the chance to cross the Atlantic and write a series of weekly impressions of what he saw - no strings attached. He could go anywhere, report anything. It all seemed too good to be true. So in April, from the elegance of South Kensington, he started preparing with enthusiastic thoroughness - from letters of introduction to guide books and extra clothes. 'London for me won't do' he said.

All his poems this spring seemed, not surprisingly, to be on severance of love ties, light or grave or both. 'The Chilterns' has touches of sophisticated humour and then there comes this:

> What's left behind I shall not find
> The splendour and the pain
> The splash of sun, the shouting wind,
> And the brave sting of rain,
> I may not meet again.

On 15 April Rupert went to the birthday party of Violet Asquith, who told him of various friends he should visit in New York.

Then when it got to the final four weeks Brooke found he had too much left to do. He saw Cathleen as often as possible; sometimes for tea in her dressing room or, when she was ill in late April, at her home. With the days dwindling they thought only of there and then.

Then suddenly the last day dawned. A pale, precious morning, lightening delicately over Kensington. He was still rushing around arranging last-night meetings and he

sent a scrawled note by hand to a friend from his home at
5 Thurloe Square:

May 20th
*I'm very sorry, I live in a whirl of mismanagement and
incompetence. I'm engaged here all day. But from 10
p.m. till midnight, I'm going to sink beer in the restaurant
under Gambrinus, Regent Street. Gibson and one or two
others will be drifting in and out.*
*And from 11.40 to 12 tomorrow I shall be dissolved in
tears on the platform at Euston. At 12 my train starts. If
you're near either of these places, do look in, if only for a
moment. If you appear tonight, I will ply you with grilled
kidneys. If I don't see you ever, in aeternium vale*
    Remember me to Locke Ellis
                R.B.

John Middleton Murry was one of those friends he saw
on the evening of 20 May. Murry, working as a journalist
and reviewer, wrote from Chancery Lane to Katherine
Mansfield that day: 'I'm going to supper with Rupert
tonight because he's going off to America in the morning;
it's all very silly, but a free meal is fascinating.'

Later Murry said that his own touch of resentment was
plain to see. There was nothing at all silly in Rupert's
going to America, nor in his asking Murry to a parting
supper. Murry was merely envious.

The evening went down in memory as one of those rare
magic moments when all is entranced, sharpened by the
proximity of parting. It was early morning before Rupert
arrived back at Thurloe Square for a few hours' sleep in
the tall grey house. Then next day to Euston, Liverpool
and the New World.

In May, Rupert started the sonnet, 'Mutability'. It must
be the poem composed over the two most distant points
possible: begun in a quiet square in South Kensington,
finished at Makaweli in the South Seas.

Poor straws! on the dark flood we catch awhile.

Mutability, in a world of change.

CHAPTER
9

Brooke boarded the SS Cedric and was led along to his cabin, number 50. He raised his eyes to the porthole. Framed in its circle he saw Birkenhead across the Mersey. He had an early evening meal and retired.

May 22 opened with grey skies. The sight of so many people on the quayside to see off friends depressed him suddenly with a sense of solitude. On an impulse Brooke hopped ashore down the main gangway, found a lad called William who was there just for interest and pressed sixpence into the palm of his small hand on the understanding that the boy would wave to him until the ship slid clear of the quay! The lad carried out his part of the pact faithfully, even shouting spontaneities quite inaudible to Brooke up on deck. Rupert, in turn, returned the waving and felt less alone as the Cedric set course westward.

Fast-scudding clouds presaged a choppy day or two as the cranes and wharves and sprawl of the Mersey moved from sight, the Irish coast faded and nothing but water lay between the Cedric and the Statue of Liberty.

Someone told Brooke that the poet Richard le Galliene and his wife were also aboard but he remained unimpressed with them and did not strike an acquaintance. His first friendship on the vessel was thrust at him by a hearty New-Century, New-World Canadian girl who kept trying to lead him into deserted corners of the ship - around lifeboats and similar spots - and then attempted to teach him her national anthem! If this failed she did succeed in getting across to him a more frivolous ditty boasting these memorable lyrics:

Splash me! Splash me! Splash me with the ocean blue.
Mash me! Mash me! and I promise that I'll mash you.

This unnerving episode occurred within the first few

days out from Liverpool and, although it amused Brooke, he was glad to get back to the safety of cabin 50. So this was a young product of the New World. Somewhat more shattering than the Newnhamites.

He also met a Mr Klaw who expressed a passionate interest in theatre. Rupert expanded his ideas on the drama and discovered that the man had major connections with several New York theatres.

Now all idea of time seemed lost and here in mid-ocean unfolded a new world - as there was to be at the other end.

The sense of strangeness which he felt, with horizons surrounding him right round the compass, was underlined by some exotic dishes - including the colourfully-named clam chowder. The prospect of this food spurred Brooke to concoct a Swinburnesque lyric for a letter to Cathleen Nesbitt:

> If you were like clam-chowder
> And I were like the spoon,
> And the band were playing louder
> And a little more in tune,
> I'd stir you till I spilled you,
> Or kiss you till I killed you,
> If you were like clam-chowder
> And I were like the spoon.

Rupert Brooke and New York. Something at once apt and yet incongruous about the two together. Already he had tasted the American outlook, for a youth on board had practically insisted on reciting the Declaration of Independence to him.

The initial impact of the New York scene from the ship surprised and inspired Brooke. The vessel passed the Statue of Liberty as evening fell and, slowly steaming in, he saw the Brooklyn Bridge, over which 'luminous trams, like shuttles of fire, are thrown across and across, continually weaving the stuff of human existence.' In the fading sky he glimpsed 'the low golden glare of Coney Island' while 'a few streamers of smoke flew over the city, oblique and parallel, pennants of our civilisation.'

Rupert read into the clusters of skyscrapers some

purpose and greatness beyond their mere convenience. Here were symbols of the century, clutching towards heaven in a ragged group. This was a moment in a million. Sundown and the restless triumphant skyline silhouetted, each spire studded with a stream of lights challenging the stars. And then, looking down into the water reflecting the remnants of this summer day, he suddenly saw that New York was real, it lived and people breathed there, for floating refuse of every kind bobbed against the hull of the ship as she edged in closer to this city of dreams - broken and real.

Yes, to the city. Rupert at large in New York, not probing too deep, just content to look and listen. The sidewalks with people chewing gum, their jaws forever moving; the security of Fifth Avenue; the floodlit toothbrush advertisements; the theatres, the movies, the elevated trains, the cars. These were what he saw, what anyone would see. Yet he observed them more closely and at the same time with detachment.

And the New Yorkers themselves - what of them? The preference of belts to braces; men not ashamed to walk about in their shirtsleeves; the latest fashion creations of Bakst; and the wonders of the department store. Most of all he noticed that scarcely any English - or American - was heard in the streets.

He was not completely captivated by New York. Its commercialism appalled him: the undertaker who included for 75 dollars 'everything that the most morbid taphologist could suggest including four draped flambeaux'!

E. S. P. Haynes gave Brooke several introductions to friends in America - one being a Swedenborgian railway king well over 80 years old! Haynes wondered at the time whether the former Swede would appreciate Rupert. He need not have worried, though, for although the two were together no more than twenty-four hours, Brooke must have made an unusual impression, for a letter from the old man to Haynes after Brooke's death showed that the Swede regarded it as a real tragedy.

Brooke wrote to Eddie Marsh, then in the Greek Islands, that New York was 'a gritty refuse-heap of reality'. Meanwhile he went on exploring the sights and decided that apart from revues, the stage shows were not exciting. No wonder Klaw had been over in London looking for fresh plays.

In early June he passed a day in the country outside the metropolis flirting with a girl named Louise, but apart from one or two such encounters he found New York a little lonely. So in mid-month he took a boat trip down the coast to Boston. Here he was struck by the simple truth that it is often far better to get a first or last impression of a place from the sea rather than by rail. Certainly it was true of Boston as he watched it rising on its little hills, looking civilised and homely after New York. In Boston he found life leisured with time for real hospitality. And still it lived although already New York had replaced it as the leading American city in the arts.

And across the river from Boston - Cambridge, Massachusetts. How could he ignore it, distant as it seemed from King's in sense and space and all dimensions? Brooke reached Cambridge, more particularly Harvard, during the University's Commencement - Eights Week and May Week and everything else in one. Here he met people he understood, a young-in-heart group with 'the charm and freshness and capacity for instantly creating a relation of happy and warm friendliness'.

The climax of the celebrations was that annual ritual, the Harvard-Yale baseball game. He settled in his seat and watched amazed the knickerbockered players, hot under the June sky; and then he saw America pass in review. The graduates of every year marched past the stands, from the 1850s down to 1912. Brooke asked a companion why there seemed to be no-one between about 50 and 60. The reply was simply: 'The war'.

However young this country and the university actually was Brooke sensed 'something• terrifying in the completeness of their lives and their civilisation ... like a company of dons whose studies are of a remote and finished world.' The subject of their scholarship was the nineteenth century and especially Victorian England. Brooke was not unduly surprised when asked if he had known Matthew Arnold and avoided explaining that Arnold had died when he was exactly eight months old!

Brooke's literary output in the month he spent in New York and Boston amounted to notes for four weekly letters to be written later for the 'Westminster Gazette' and eight lonely lines of verse, 'There's a Wisdom in Women'. This could be sold for a guinea he told Marsh in a covering letter.

On the last day but one in June he left America for Canada, 'a country without a soul' American friends warned him when they heard of his intention. Defying these cries he took the Montreal Express out of New York at 7.45 p.m. on the night of the 29th.

As usual Rupert had rushed round the city saying farewell to the friends he had made there, so ate nothing all day. Only as the train exploded out of the station did he discover that it had no restaurant car aboard and his last memory of the United States for almost a year was munching an orange and still feeling hungry after it. With the sweet tang still in his mouth he clambered gracefully into a lofty sleeping berth, directly above an old lady who was snoring almost before the train crossed the Hudson River.

Then, propped up in bed, he pulled back one of the two little curtains at the window, relaxed back on to his elbow and peeped into the black night. Faintly he made out the surface of a large lake lying away behind the trees. It was all strange beyond belief. Glimpses of shapes and places he had never seen, nor ever would. The world was passing him by in darkness. At last he tired of looking out towards the racing landscape and thought of the more familiar sights. He started a letter to Eddie Marsh, barely legible with the motion of the train, and spoke in fun of his mental stupor in America. The pace and the people apparently did not inspire any lasting lyrics. Perhaps it was all too far away; or not far enough.

The night wore away and in the early hours Brooke fell fitfully asleep as the express raced round the clock and crossed into Canada. Then a miracle. Early next morning, as he was grappling to get his trousers on in an upper berth, he pulled a curtain open again to see the train running beside a huge sunlit river, the splendid St. Lawrence curving crystal blue in the sparkling new day. Everything had changed. It was a world - not just a night - away from New York. Soon the outlook switched to squalor as the poorer parts of Montreal blurred row and row past the window.

Rupert set out to see Montreal by wagonette observation-car in company with a score of tourists and found an 'atmospheric' similarity to Glasgow. A city of banks and churches, he found it terribly tedious and delayed only a day or two.

He would be going on to Ottawa soon but before this, he caught the night boat from Montreal to Quebec. The vessel left the gloom of Montreal and swung into the sweeping St. Lawrence. On board Brooke met a middle-aged American Jew, also travelling more or less aimlessly. This man said everything he thought but, despite his transparent mind, he became an agreeable companion to Rupert for a day or two. They awoke after the night on the river to a perfect midsummer morning and there, high above, stood the citadel of Quebec, dominant on its headland in the course of the water. A youthful city, he saw it with 'the radiance and repose of an immortal'.

Rupert took a calèche, a little local two-wheeled carriage, and together with the American he saw where Wolfe fell and all the other points of historic renown. The American burst into a slightly off-key rendering of 'The Star-Spangled Banner' as they jogged past his national consulate! Soon he settled down to sleep while the carriage rocked them along narrower and still narrower streets paved with planks.

Brooke liked it here. Alone on another day he paused on Dufferin Terrace to sit and stare at the Lower Town, backed by the river, the citadel and the Isle of Orleans. 'Hour by hour, the colours change, and sunlight follows shadow, and mist rises, and smoke drifts across.' He also wrote to Eddie Marsh from this perfect point close to the House of Parliament. When a man and two girls came and sat nearby, he had 'a slight lust' for one of them as she looked so graceful and neat in the red and white outfit.

Once more the colours changed, the moment passed.

He took another river trip which he had been recommended: 130 miles down the St. Lawrence, 90 miles up a tributary, the Saguenay, and then back to Quebec. After passing a host of tiny French hamlets alongside the river the boat finally reached the junction with the Saguenay. The St. Lawrence here is twenty miles wide and the boat turned into the tributary during darkness, so that the narrowness and the night combined to convey an oppressive sense to the dim outlines of vast cliffs following their course.

Back at the junction of the rivers again, Brooke stopped for a day at the village there called Tadousac. In this remote spot he felt the full desolation of the river which faded out of sight across its wide span. The sun beat down hotly so Rupert stripped off his clothes, hesitated a second and plunged in. Despite the summer, the water was icy. He swam for only a couple of minutes, before striking back to land and scrambling on to the hot rocks. He patted himself dry with a handkerchief, dressed and ran all the way back to the little log hotel, still shivering, his hair gleaming gold in the sunlight.

At Ottawa the money motive was not all. Here Brooke sensed more civilised surroundings than Montreal where statistics and size had seemed much more important to the people than art or culture. Even in Ottawa, however, he felt unable to record fine, clear impressions. He had visualised himself composing at a prolific rate once he was 'dancing through foreign cities' but the brain did not respond! The normally sensitive reactions were not forthcoming. Still, he liked the grace of Ottawa and the soft Canadian accents heard in its streets. And one considerable compensation was the hospitality shown to him by the Canadian poet Duncan Campbell Scott.

John Masefield had given Brooke a letter of introduction to Scott and also to the Canadian prime minister, Sir Wilfred Laurier, with whom he lunched. It was Scott who really entertained Brooke for the next week. Rupert was registered at an Ottawa hotel but spent all the time at Scott's home. Although the Canadian was twice Brooke's age, they got along well, with poetry in common and were photographed together in the garden. Scott wore rimless spectacles and sat in a modern-looking broad-striped summer chair with a kitten in his lap, while Rupert balanced a teacup on the wide arm of a wooden chair. Brooke, for once, wore a high wing collar and his hair fell over his forehead towards his left eye.

He took most of his meals either with the Scotts or at the Royal Ottawa Golf Club and as the week passed he grew less lonely than when he had reached the capital. They coaxed him to read poems from 'Georgian Poetry' and his own recent work, and discussed literature at length with him.

Scott thought Brooke not only handsome but that everything about him went together harmoniously. His last memory of the eight days Brooke spent in Ottawa was typical: Rupert lying on his back on the rug in Scott's library playing with the kitten.

Before Brooke said adieu he took Scott to the Golf Club house for drinks. Here with whisky and soda they toasted poetry, for Rupert described Scott as 'the only poet in Canada'. As the Canadian was to visit England in the autumn, Rupert wrote to friends asking them to welcome him appropriately.

Just before leaving Ottawa, Brooke took a twenty-mile excursion out of it by motor car over dusty tracks to a lovely lake in the hills away to the north-west. Beside the rough road grew mildweed, cornflowers, thimbleberry blossom, and purple-red fireweed. He breathed air as clear and clean as the visibility and felt excited, elated, that the North Pole lay straight ahead with scarcely any civilisation between it and him.

With that thought he returned to Ottawa but only to take to the water once more for his next call - Toronto. The boat picked a channel through the famous Thousand Isles. Brooke was not impressed. 'Each, if big enough, has been bought by a rich man - generally an American - who has built a castle on it. So the whole isn't much more beautiful than Golders Green.'

Toronto at last, on the shores of the lake. However the unfortunate people scarcely saw it as the waterfront was occupied by smoke, stores, railways and wharves.

Despite this prospect, Rupert noted here the beginnings of art - but only the beginnings. The first repertory theatre in Canada, he prophesied, would be founded in Toronto some thirty years hence, and would daringly present 'Candida' and 'The Silver Box'!

What can one say about Toronto? 'It is impossible to give it anything but commendation. It is not squalid like Birmingham, or cramped like Canton, or scattered like Edmonton, or sham like Berlin, or hellish like New York, or tiresome like Nice. It is all right. The only depressing thing is that it will always be what it is, only larger, and that no Canadian city can ever be anything better or different. If they are good they may become Toronto.'

Despite this penetrating analysis Brooke felt some sympathy for the place. Duncan Scott gave him an introduction to the Arts and Letters Club where he met men who were very kind to him. Two of them bore the homely names of Morris and McTavish. Edmund Morris, a noted painter of Indians, shepherded Brooke to the Club, then housed in the old Assize Court of Toronto. A poetry lover, Rufus Hathaway, at the club that first night had already read Rupert's poems in 'Georgian Poetry'. Another man owned a copy of his poems. Awful triumph, Brooke told Marsh.

'You're better than Alfred Noyes, in my opinion' someone else volunteered.

So here among artists, poets and journalists Brooke felt more at home than in any other city so far. He wrote regularly to no-one now, not even his 'four young women' - presumably the Olivier girls. Noel and the New Forest seemed centuries ago and even Cathleen Nesbitt filled his mind less. A strange, complicated thing was life. Not so simple just to be happy. Perhaps the most elusive of all. Next day, he set out from the King Edward Hotel, Toronto, for the wilds and the West: Winnipeg and on to Vancouver. First he had to see Niagara.

Two days later, writing to Marsh from the Clifton Hotel, Niagara, he described the Falls as low and broad and gloomy. Then with typical originality of thought he said he was hearing the same noise as George Washington, only a little later on. The hotels, bridges, trams, postcards, sideshows and all the touts of all kinds there he deplored deeply. Then he admitted the power of the falls, and that 'he who sees them instantly forgets humanity'. Brooke watched the spray ranging from diaphanous to dark and thought of the river of life, with many flashing moments within a single stream.

By boat now through Lakes Huron and Superior. On the Sunday the journey started they passed picnic parties and others ashore, looking so happy that Brooke felt the way of life here had a fine, breezy, enviable healthiness.

Then the boat moved past a small canoe with a red-shirted man and a bronzed girl. The voyagers whistled, sang and shouted 'snooky-ookums' to the pair, much to Rupert's amusement.

He was sitting next to an old lady on deck who would raise a massive telescope to her eye every few minutes, aim it at a distant shore and if she saw signs of life there, wave her tiny handkerchief - though no-one could possibly have seen it at that range!

Ashore again and by night train in a lower sleeping berth. He got between the sheets, pulled up the blinds a few inches and watched the woods and hills of the wild starlit landscape make a mingled night of dream and reality. Early next morning, the train roared into Winnipeg and the West.

Here he found 'a tempered democracy' and architecture more hideous than in the east, 'but cheerily and windily so'. In compensation Western manners seemed better than back East.

The wilds suited him better than Winnipeg itself so he found a friend and headed for a far-off lodge at Lake George, seventy miles north. Here in the wilderness and waste he mused that no-one else was *thinking* of the lakes and hills he saw before him. They had no tradition these places, often no names. All was still virginal, untrodden, rare. Dawn followed sunset with an infinite loneliness - and a loveliness too.

He was here on his twenty-sixth birthday, lying naked on a beach of golden sand. He lay and thought and remembered. The past was over. The future unreal. And the present? This should have meant something. But did it? What was the meaning of it all? Back at the hunting lodge he wrote to Cathleen telling her how they had landed at a place which was an Indian camp. The complete contrast - from Brooke in the backwoods of Manitoba to Cathleen Nesbitt in her Shaftesbury Avenue world.

Pressing westwards, on relentlessly to Regina. The children in the same carriage kept on demanding: How many inches to Regina? A billion? A trillion? A shillion? Past the Prairies, vast, vastly lonely.

Two other passengers in the corner argued about the

merits and size of their respective home-towns of Edmonton and Calgary. Each vied with the other about the rate of growth. Then for a change one of them turned to Rupert and asked:

'Say, where do you come from, friend?'

Rupert had to admit to them that Grantchester, having numbered 300 at the time of Julius Caesar, rising to nearly 400 by Domesday Book, had now dropped to 350 in the year of grace 1913. They seemed 'perplexed and angry', Rupert reported!

By 13 August he was at Edmonton, three-quarters across Canada, where he wrote telling Eddie Marsh that he had become the complete journalist, demanding free passes and bursting in on people for interviews.

Back in the East he had been regarded as a poet, but three days later at Calgary he was a political expert - and reporters started interviewing *him*! Columns appeared in the local papers reporting his opinions on the situation in Europe and other topics. Brooke told Marsh that he would demand a knighthood from Winston when he came back!

From Calgary Rupert saw the Rockies rising seventy miles away. 'They are irrelevant to humanity' he concluded. No recorded Hannibal has ever struggled across them; nor is their story in any remembered literature.

On again, towards these giants. Sitting in the observation car at the rear of the train westward he likened the carriage to life. You never saw the glories until they were past. Through the Rockies themselves. Banff he found ordinary, though beautiful enough.

Yet Lake Louise was another world. Here in the Selkirk mountains, amid milky green waters reflecting peaks and pines, he met an alluring widow - the Lady of the Chateau - who helped him to pass an idyllic few days. So it was people not places that really mattered.

Across the Great Divide and there at last lay Vancouver, surrounded by mountains and with an air of the Orient about it. Passing south, to the States and San Francisco, he discovered with alarm that he had lost his precious notebook containing all the impressions of his Canadian travels, so he could do little except write the rest of the articles for the 'Westminster Gazette' from memory.

118

The American ones had been safely despatched earlier.

September sped by in the friendly setting of the University of California at Berkeley, where he found himself positively revered, not for his own abilities so much as his associations with such legendary Englishmen as John Masefield. Names like these seemed unbelievably remote to the students at Berkeley, a continent and an ocean away from England.

Brooke liked California and the easy companionship of a young state. San Francisco was just recovering from the fire of 1906 and everything looked new and touched with gold. Meanwhile, he took this opportunity to clear up his affairs in case he decided to go still further into the unexplored. Any completed poems he posted to Marsh and half-finished ones he hoped to find peace to finish.

In a note to Dr Dent Brooke was still wondering whether to go on or not, as he thought of Cambridge, 'that lovely grey city of ours'. Eventually he tossed a coin to decide: heads for home, tails for the Pacific. He flicked an American dollar into the air, caught it in one hand and slowly uncovered his fingers to see which it would be. There it was in his hand - tails.

So on 1 October he wrote to Eddie Marsh saying that he would be sailing for Honolulu in a few days - picturing himself in the centre of a Gauguin painting nakedly riding a squat horse into white surf: how lucky the coin came down right or he would never have written his poems from the South Seas.

The ship sailed south-west from San Francisco and all at once the utter remoteness of the Pacific swept over Rupert. As if the world were flat and they were early voyagers heading towards its edge, not knowing where or when they might see land again.

Among the passengers were some Hawaiians returning home. They gave him a foretaste of the South Seas with their soft, slumbrous lovesongs, chanted to chords from strings on the mild autumn air. Several of the Hawaiian girls looked longingly at the strangely beautiful Englishman but he had not yet succumbed to the mesmeric charm of the islands.

During these first few days and nights that the ship cut calmly through the Pacific Rupert wrote two of his South Seas poems: the sonnets 'He Wonders Whether' and 'Clouds'. The former had no particular connection with the place or period except that he said:

I have peace to weigh your worth, now all is over

'Clouds' was a direct inspiration from communion with the Pacific skies. Accomplished as much of his previous work was, this marked a new degree of mastery over the sonnet, with its exquisite opening lines:

Down the blue night the unending columns press
In noiseless tumult, break and wave and flow

Two thousand miles - and Honolulu about the middle of the month. From here he sent a small group of poems to Eddie Marsh, four of which were at once re-directed to 'Poetry and Drama': 'He Wonders Whether'; 'Clouds'; 'The Funeral of Youth'; and 'The Way that Lovers Use'. So the two sonnets he had written in early October on the other side of the world reached home and appeared in print within two months of their conception.

Honolulu seemed terribly Americanised to Brooke, who could not enthuse over it. Nevertheless, from Waikiki Beach, where he stayed for some days, he wrote two more sonnets, suggesting that a surrender to the Islands must have begun. From one:

> Somewhere before the dawn I rose, and stept
> Softly along the dim way to your room

And in 'Waikiki" -

> Somewhere an eukaleli thrills and cries
> And stabs with pain the night's brown savagery

He had tasted the pure pagan life and it appealed to him, for there ran a strong vein of the primitive in his highly sensitive make-up. This was another world he was discovering, infinitely different from England and all civilisation. The barriers were down, inhibitions gone. Yet he was torn between the two; he had not yet let go. In 'One Day' he wrote:

> Today I have been happy. All the day
> remembering the past in England.

They crossed the Equator near Phoenix Islands and another few days brought them to Samoa. He had sent nine articles back to the 'Westminster Gazette' before leaving San Francisco; now he was too engrossed, engulfed, with the wonder of the South Seas to do more.

It was all true what they said about these parts. The heaven here on earth; lovely natives; tropic climate; perfect settings. He fell for the thatched roofs of the homes, and the palms dark against the morning light. From a Samoan grass hut he wrote to Cathleen, who was still -

> Lucretia, Helen, Mary, in one breath!

Brooke saw the lithe grace of the girls, a beautiful brown, free from any 'Melanesian admixture'. He told

121

Denis Browne that he was becoming more and more Robert Louis Stevenson and at this stage actually wondered when or even if he would ever return north again. While at Samoa he made a pilgrimage to Stevenson's grave at Vailima, where the Scotsman had been buried nineteen years earlier.

Brooke became bronzed and tough and life was one long picnic. Yet even at the outposts he saw the signs of civilisation. At a remote village one of the chiefs had a passion for collecting pictures from 'The Sketch'! He used to cut out illustrations and nail them to the beams of his hut, which was thus decorated with a strange assortment of fashion photos, a golf champion in the act of driving and portraits of stage and social celebrities. In one of the cuttings Rupert came across a picture of Cathleen. London to Samoa. Now, as he looked at her cultured beauty, it was the periodical and its world which seemed unreal. Did it actually exist? London, fogs, King's, Cathleen, Eddie Marsh. Were they all living their lives away this very moment? It must be so, yet reality seemed to be here, in this hut on a Samoan beach, where the sun blazed and the surf played perpetually the song of peace.

At last, saturated with Samoa, he moved on from its coconuts and waterfalls to Fiji where, to his utter disgust, he found a flourishing township complete with bookmakers! Despite this temporary interruption to primitive paganism Brooke was realising reluctantly the dangers as well as the delights of a soporific Pacific existence. He felt afraid at times that he would soon stop serious thought altogether - already he had expressed a preference for a Siva-Siva dance rather than Nijinski. Six men and six girls, naked to the waist, against an exciting background of flaming torches, moving to plangent rhythms under the stars.

So to Suva with its hibiscus wreaths for the hair, the sleek canoes threading through depth-clear waters with their turtles and tropic fish. Brooke had an attachment to water, whether the chuckling mill at Grantchester or the Fijian sea. It was while here that he completed that little satiric cameo 'Heaven', a fishy paradise where -

There shall be no more land, say Fish.

On 1 December 1913, while at McDonald's Hotel, Suva, he had his first real yearnings to be home. Later they subsided for several months. As a way out of his dilemma he was evolving a pattern of life when he could live a quarter of each year with Jacques and Gwen Raverat, Dudley and Anne Ward, the Ranee (Mrs Brooke) and the last three months alone. 'Won't 1914 be fun,' he ended a letter. However he was still sufficiently happy here, so the dilemma remained.

When he was content - most of the time - he would adorn his letters with sketches such as the one to Denis Browne, the musician. In it he depicted himself sitting on top of the world, while Browne, in a blackened area, hammered away at the keys in the underworld of England at the bottom of the globe. Then, in mock-sad mood, he splashed the sheets with 'tear-stains' denoting how he felt to be away from friends. What were his real feelings? A mixture some way between these two poles.

In the early part of December he was among the angry mountains of Fiji, buffeted by thunderstorms, threatened by volcanoes. By the middle of the month he was departing - to the sincere sorrow of many of the people there, who had been as usual attracted by his charm. One of the friends he had made was a towering native guide, Ambele, who wore only a loin cloth and a giant grin.

The last outward port of call came now. Auckland at its midsummer, a week before Christmas. Rupert ate dishes of strawberries feeling as if it were some ghastly perversion or sin! The country of New Zealand impressed him only as rather dull and grey after the tropic-strong shades of the islands. Despite its Liberal or Fabian way of life it still seemed very much less than paradise - far worse than the natural anarchy of the Pacific. Which was better? Things got perplexing sometimes. Meanwhile he had two or three weeks before a boat was due to take him to Tahiti. He tidied up one or two poems already roughed out and enclosed a couple on 16 January when he next wrote to Marsh from Tahiti. These were 'Heaven' and the immortal sonnet:

Not with vain tears, when we're beyond the sun,
  We'll beat on the substantial doors, nor tread

Those dusty high-roads of the aimless dead
Plaintive for earth; but rather turn and run

Brooke added that Gauguin grossly maligned the
Tahitian ladies! The mood of the island lay heavy upon
him after only a day or so there. The moon was on the
lagoon and it was too warm for writing he told Marsh. He
would go and dream and float and woo nymphs.

Eddie Marsh wrote to tell him that 'Georgian Poetry'
had entered its ninth impression in triumph. About the
same time Brooke heard of the progress in the plan to
publish a quarterly poetry periodical. The original
intention had been to christen this 'The Gallows Garland'
after Lascelles Abercrombie's Gloucester cottage home.
The organisers decided that this sounded too grim and
might prove bad for business, so settled on the more
innocuous title of 'New Numbers'. The first of these
quarterly garlands appeared in February 1914 with works
by Abercrombie, Drinkwater, Gibson and Brooke. The
remarkable thing about it was that although the quarterly
was published from Ryton in Gloucestershire it included
'Not with Vain Tears' posted by Rupert from Tahiti only a
month earlier! His other three contributions to this first
number were 'A Memory', 'One Day' and 'Mutability.'

As 'New Numbers' came out, Brooke forwarded a
further 'few things' as he put it. These comprised a
priceless quartet: 'The Great Lover', 'Retrospect',
'Hauntings', and 'Tiare Tahiti'. The former two he wrote
in Mateia; 'Hauntings' he composed while en route to
Tahiti and finished off there; 'Tiare Tahiti' he wrote in its
main town of Papeete.

After a week or so in Papeete, he withdrew some thirty
miles along the coast to Mateia which was a wonderful
spot for working or lazing. Once more Rupert sensed the
overwhelming attraction of the Pacific surroundings, their
fatalistic philosophy, perhaps purer and simpler than his
complex civilisation. At Mateia he sat on a wide veranda,
shaded from the sun, overlooking a rich blue lagoon. Here
he stretched out his legs and turned his mind to the good
things of the earth elsewhere, as well as on Tahiti, and
wrote -

Here he wrote the last four of his Canadian articles for the 'Westminster Gazette'. And here he made love.

In Tahiti everyone wore a white flower behind their ears, but it was whether the left or the right - or both - which was the important thing. Behind the right ear meant they were looking for a sweetheart; behind the left, they had found one; behind both, they were looking for a second! Brooke saw the allure that the island must have had for Gauguin who had lived his last ten years there a decade earlier.

Rupert realised only too well how, once settled there, the days and weeks would drift into months and years, till the will to return would be gone forever. He was wise or restless enough not to grow tied to that extent, for he knew in his heart he missed the enlivening influence of Europe. Yet his dilemma was still sufficiently real, for he saw how much more honest was this tropic-sand life than the parade of pseudo-intelligentsia or the merely moribund encountered in England! It was only the thought of his real friends that swayed the scales.

In February he completed 'Tiare Tahiti'. In it he seemed still clearly under the Pacific influence but this could not be wholly bad if it were capable of stimulating such idyllic images. Once more it reveals the curious complex. If he believed the beauty he found at Tahiti why did he want to leave? Probably only because he would always want to move on from any place after as long as he had spent here. Three months on one island was a long time indeed. So the little land of Gauguin and Captain Bligh seeped into him.

The turning-point came when he contracted a form of coral-poisoning - intensified by bathing. The illness brought home to him his vagabondage. He told Erica Cotterill all about his poisoned legs and how he was being nursed by a girl 'with wonderful eyes'. In his passing depression he admitted that he had lost a dream or two in trying to be a poet. Perhaps, he felt, he had been given some talent but not quite enough. He thought he had missed greatness and also let the world slip by him. He had seen fish and skies the colour of a rainbow; waves breaking in glistening line on hot golden sand; a radiant brown girl on a green and purple reef. What was left? What could come after the scarlet dawns, the cooling winds? England was two worlds away: from the Pacific to America, then across the Atlantic.

As April came alike to Tahiti and Grantchester, Rupert sailed from the surrender of the islands, back to San Francisco. *Partir, c'est toujours mourir un peu.* He felt this acutely as he leaned over the rail and followed the wake of the ship straight back to the bay and his eyes looked up and beyond the green coast and Papeete to the jutting peaks of the hills, ringed in clouds. How wonderful these people were and how much they meant to him. He told them he would return.

CHAPTER
11

San Francisco rose all around the bay like an arm waiting to imprison him. Brooke hated its houses and public conveyances and worst of all - the need to wear a collar! For a few days he stayed with friends at Berkeley and then he realised that although he might look healthy, he was also wild and woolly! After eleven months on the move his clothes had frayed and he had little money left. All he got for the 'Westminster Gazette' articles was four guineas per piece.

So he decided it was time to head east again. Leaving California he actually went south-east to take in the Grand Canyon and the rugged wastes of Arizona.

High on a plateau with a coat to protect him against spring snow Rupert sat and stared away in the distance, then down at the mile-deep drop inside the canyon. For six or seven miles on each side the great cliffs of rock rose stark, primeval. Unlike his soul, he thought, it had peace in it. The wind whipped the snow into a whirl of whiteness suddenly blotting out the whole scene. Then he stepped down from this vastness back into a world of surprising culture, for he met friends of the serious theatre in Chicago, of all places.

Rupert registered at the Auditorium Hotel, and then, as he had been thinking more about the theatre on the journey home, he scribbled a note to Maurice Browne, whom Harold Munro had said was' a moving force in the experimental drama of America. Browne was running the Chicago Little Theatre which had its headquarters next door to Brooke's Hotel, in the Fine Arts Building. Brooke and Browne had been chasing each other for two years before this day in the third week of April when they finally met.

Browne read the note on his arrival at the theatre and at once telephoned asking Brooke to come round and meet them all. In a couple of minutes Rupert was walking along the sidewalk, hurrying into the neighbouring building.

Brooke had no idea that Chicago was so culturally advanced, although he did know of Harriet Monroe's magazine 'Poetry'. All the arts flourished in the mid-west during this exciting era. Ben Hecht was one of the producers trying out ideas in the Little Theatre at this time.

Maurice Browne had been born and educated in England but had come out to the United States to start this ardent group, whose whole lives revolved around the courageous Little Theatre. To Brooke they were people of his very own and he extended his original itinerary of only three or four days in Chicago, which he had imagined to be hellish, to ten.

This week-and-a-half merged itself into an endless, riotous blur of all-night talks, club sandwiches and then the dawn, chill-clean over Lake Michigan. Rupert was entranced with the theatre and rhapsodised over it, then suddenly he would be withdrawn for a while. Yet speaking or silent, he spent practically his whole ten days there while they were rehearsing.

Browne was an actor as well as producer and his wife, Ellen Van Volkenburg, played leading roles. After the day's rehearsing they returned to their studio, a few blocks south overlooking the lake, and here Brooke showed them all his South Seas treasures. He presented Ellen with several delicate chains made of Pacific shells.

'Why, they're beautiful, Rupert' she cried excitedly, fastening them around her neck as she rushed over to look in the property mirror on the wall. He also gave her a copy of Hilaire Belloc's 'Four Men' which he seemed to know almost by heart! Then the three of them sat up night after night talking, singing folk-songs, reading poetry, creating their own world in a setting of one chair, a table and some packing cases - they did not have much money. This was what Rupert had missed and now he really wondered why he had been so hesitant to leave the Islands.

On three successive mornings they saw the sun inching up, a misty flame sphere on the still lake. Then they went to bed for a few hours, rising for an 11 a.m. breakfast.

One special night Maurice lured into the studio group

an Iowa poet and attorney, Arthur Davison Ficke. The bait which Browne offered was 'poetry, beer and Brooke'. Ficke bit it firmly for like Browne he had already read Rupert's Poems. So started one of those memorable nights of declamation, discussion, disagreement - on free verse, rhyming, writing for the theatre and anything else. Ficke came, saw and fell under the spell of the incomparable Brooke personality, later celebrating the event in a sonnet, 'Portrait of Rupert Brooke'.

They persuaded Rupert to read his poems to them, almost all he had written, including 'Lithuania' and the South Seas works. The group sat still as statues, Ficke in the decrepit rocker, the others sprawled over odd pieces of furniture. Rupert read with his usual mellifluence, the soft slight stress of rhythm and rhyme. His tones touched each one of them as they heard this flow of lyric verse from a voice in the night. And as Rupert reached 'Tiare Tahiti' all Chicago seemed asleep and the room suspended in space and time, an island oasis in the ocean of the poem.

The days fled. Maurice was so impressed with 'Lithuania' that he wanted to produce it, but both he and Ellen were due to visit England and the idea had to be postponed. They were due to sail a week after Brooke but Rupert decided to accompany them and he set about planning it. Meanwhile, he continued his Chicago stay and his long legs strode freely down the sidewalks. In his right hand he swung a broad-brimmed, high-crowned, featherweight hat, which was plaited from South Seas straw, and so a precious possession. The wind blew the Chicago dust and cinders through his hair but he did not mind. He was in his own world again.

Rupert went to Washington during the first week of May with the intention of meeting his 'Lady of the Chateau'. On 10 May he wrote to Browne from the capital asking if he could travel over on the same boat as them. Browne told him they would be sailing on the Philadelphia from New York on the 29th, but Brooke did not get this immediately as he was now in New Jersey en route for 'Bawston' having fled from Pittsburgh in terror! Finally, though, he was able to fix a berth on the Philadelphia.

Once in Boston, he hurried over to Harvard for a

return visit to the university and met a guest lecturer there from England for the summer term. This proved to be Bertrand Russell, his brilliant friend from the days of Cambridge and the Apostles. Here in the newer Cambridge the two met again with the campus at its spring best. Brooke was in top form and Russell remembered his handsome and bronzed features specially well.

Earl Russell told me how Rupert arrived wearing his South Seas hat, and a certain Professor Perry wondered who on earth the strange young man was. Brooke started to expound in fun the theory that the South Seas had lapsed into a state of decadence ever since cannibalism had ceased there, twenty or so years earlier! As he proceeded, Perry became more and more shocked, not realising that it was all humorous, and afterwards turned to Russell saying: 'I don't think he should talk about cannibalism at all - let alone speak in favour of it!'

Perry did not know, of course, that this was Rupert's favourite funny topic in his correspondence home from the Pacific, nor that he had written a sonnet on it as well, opening:

The limbs that erstwhile charmed your sight
Are now a savage's delight;

One of Bertrand Russell's pupils at Harvard that term was T. S. Eliot, who heard his whole course of lectures. There is no record of any meeting between Brooke and Eliot, although it is quite possible.

Brooke got to New York the week before sailing date and stayed at the Hotel McAlpin, Greeley Square. Here he received a set of portraits taken by the Chicago photographer, Eugene Hutchinson. Unfortunately a middle-aged lady's pictures had been forwarded to Rupert in error for his own, but an exchange of letters remedied this.

So 29 May dawned and he met the Brownes under the shadow of the ship. Ellen Van Volkenburg said that Brooke was looking very fit and Rupertish and was carrying his straw hat, an overcoat, Hutchinson's photographs, some magazines, books and a writing case. His arrival on board caused a *succès de scandale*!

130

Tucked away on deck, Rupert found Ellen with a pen in hand. 'Are you writing to your mother? May I add a line at the end please?' He scrawled his own message on hers: *Ave atque vale.*

Then the ship left the majesty of Manhattan, a year to the day after the SS Cedric had arrived there, bringing Brooke on his travels. He felt much more than a year older. Still young in heart but beyond his twenty-six years.

The trio settled down to enjoy a week aboard the liner and then a June homecoming at Plymouth. The voyage went well. After dinner on the first full day out, they played three-handed bridge and then strolled round the deck in the sea starlight. Next day, they saw for the tenth time a small podgy girl whom Brooke had christened playfully 'the pig child'. Ellen wondered what he would have called her in childhood days.

The three of them continued the game of naming suitably the more outrageous people on board. Two sisters aged about 20 and 22, who had their eyes on every man in sight, Rupert adorned as Mimi and Fifi.

Ellen recorded that Brooke was having sighs and eyes cast at him and even a married woman took a snapshot of him because - as she said - he had such a noble head. Two tables down from their own, a young girl gazed at him dumbfounded and 'beautifully melancholy'.

Just after the halfway mark they met a painter, Ronald Hargreave, and on 3 June spent most of the day in his cabin working on his idea for projecting scenery on to the backdrop of a stage by painting a miniature landscape on glass and putting it in a projector. Brooke had heard of this idea before and was keen to explore its possibilities.

Later on, the three men decided to write sonnets and settled into a businesslike attitude to do so. Hargreave achieved one or two but threw them overboard in disgust! Brooked dashed off a pretentious pair entitled 'The True Beatitude' and 'Plato was Right'. Then later still in the library, to the inspiration of beer and lemonade, Maurice, Rupert and Ellen composed a ballad, each writing alternate lines. This started symbolically:

Sing not of California, no!

Now they were a mere twenty-four hours out of Plymouth where they were due to berth about 6.30 p.m. The day ended triumphantly with a Marconigram from Eddie Marsh inviting them all to dine with him in his rooms.

Land's End and the Lizard loomed and faded as 5 June dragged by. In the afternoon Ellen joined Brooke at the taffrail and found him sniffing ecstatically the scent of new-mown hay from the fields near the east Cornwall cliffs. Together they watched the mellow brown and green landscape take shape and once more Rupert told her that he still loved Cathleen Nesbitt and would see her as soon as he could.

As the two of them were leaning over the rail looking down at the water, they suddenly heard a noise behind them. They turned their heads sharply and a camera clicked. Then a woman came up and asked in an embarrassed way who they were. They answered 'Brooke-Browne' whereupon she volunteered that she was enquiring for the friend who had taken the photograph and simply had to know, as they looked quite the most interesting people on board and seemed to be having such a good time. They assured her that they were the most interesting - and did have a good time!

Rupert found out that the Russian Ballet was on in London so the Brownes decided to defer a projected Paris trip for a while. They had plans to operate an English theatre in the French capital.

The Philadelphia docked on time and they saw Rupert off on the London train, arranging to meet the following week. While Brooke had been abroad, he had visualised the route the train would follow and he dozed content to know that it was steaming through the West Country night, past Teignmouth, with its connections with Keats, Exeter and on across Wiltshire.

Finally he stirred, to see the shape of Paddington curving into view at the dead of night. He leapt out of the carriage, trotted down the platform still carrying his hat and at 2.45 a.m. on the morning of 6 June was met by wild shrieks from Eddie Marsh, Denis Browne and Cathleen Nesbitt. He flung his arms around Cathleen. He was home.

CHAPTER

12

Eight wild weeks followed. After only a few hours' sleep, Rupert rushed on to Rugby. 'Must pay my respects to the Ranee,' he told them. He got home the same afternoon, Saturday 6 June, and assured his mother that all was well. 'I can only stay two or three days now' he admitted, 'because Eddie Marsh has booked seats for the Russian Ballet on Thursday with Maurice Browne and Ellen - the two I met in Chicago.'

Mrs Brooke was not really surprised. She had got beyond that by now. She contented herself just knowing that he was alive and happy, realising her world and his seemed planets apart. Rupert wrote to tell the Brownes about Thursday and arranged to meet them as they were comparative strangers to London.

The night of 11 June was to be yet another of those unforgettable times. Brooke came up from the smoke of Rugby; the Brownes got to London promptly, too; and they all dined out with Eddie Marsh and Cathleen before going on to the ballet. Marsh had been lucky to get tickets, which were almost unobtainable anywhere, so the five of them appreciated it all the more. Almost as soon as they sat down they saw some of the legendary London figures who were there as well; Arnold Bennett, Queen Alexandra and the Bernard Shaws.

It was the ballet which was all-important. The moment when the conductor's baton flicked up and the lights went down. The magic moment of expectant silence. Then the music sounded and the first of the two ballets of the evening began. 'Les Papillons' and then 'Petrouchka'. Fokine had given way as choreographer to the fabulous Nijinski. Rupert gazed at the scene spellbound by its beauty. This was life. Now he really felt back among the living and civilisation again. The Russian Ballet and his old and new friends. He glanced sideways to reassure himself. Yes, this was really Cathleen beside him. Her provocative profile darkly silhouetted in the reflection from the footlights. And Eddie, dear Eddie, with Maurice and Ellen on the other side. This was how it would be always, he thought. He'd been a fool to be away for so long, exiled on those islands. Always? Or just for the next few weeks till August. Here he was at his zenith, more mature yet still with his delightful humour, gentleness, modesty. 'We shall not see again the mixture of elements which made him.' Rupert sat there entranced, as the butterflies spread their wings; then the tragic beauty of Petrouchka, the sad-faced clown puppet and his hopeless love for Ballerina. Rupert saw some parallel to his own life but tonight he really felt too gay for tears. The evening passed in a flash of feet, colour, movement, music and suddenly they were outside Covent Garden, walking along Floral Street in the fresh, fragrant June air. The night had not yet really begun: this night that they would all remember.

'Come on back to Raymond Buildings', Eddie invited them.

About 11.15, as well as the ballet party, a whole host of other friends descended on the rooms in Gray's Inn to welcome Rupert back from his wanderings. It was a surprise planned by Eddie Marsh. Norman Wilkinson, Alfred Rothenstein, Granville Barker with his wife Lillah McCarthy, Henry Ainley, Harold Monro, Wilfrid Gibson, Basil Dean and others! Fiesta flared into life as midnight chimed across the Inn. The noise grew to a tumult.

Here was a cross-section of poetry, painting and the theatre ready to open their arms again to Brooke. And through the scene like a dream moved the exquisite Cathleen Nesbitt: too intelligent an actress to be merely a star. The Brownes found it all dreamlike too, especially the chilling nectar of iced coffee produced at the psychological moment by Marsh's master cook!

In one night, Brooke took up practically every string he had dropped a year before. He talked animatedly, passionately, to everyone, especially Basil Dean. Among the guests tirelessly flitted the figure of Eddie himself, his high-pitched voice and birdlike manner covering keen pleasure at having mustered all these brilliant people under one roof - his own.

Back to Basil Dean, who had come to act in London from Liverpool. Marsh had liked Dean's performance and got in touch with him through Galsworthy. Dean was then appearing in 'The Silver Box' and soon found himself drawn into that charmed circle of Eddie's, through whom he met Gordon Bottomley, Ivor Novello, then in the extreme youth of his promise, and now Brooke. Marsh had become the paterfamilias of this entire group of young artists seeking release from the complacent materialism of the recent Edwardian era. Things were certainly stirring on the Georgian scene.

Dean and Brooke agreed with each other from that first meeting. They sat on the stone stairs outside the main room - there was scarcely anywhere else to go - and talked in excited, staccato tones of the new drama they both supported so much. Dean yearned for his castle in the air, a new theatre devoted to the worthwhile dramatic art. He had neither the money nor the access to it - only a fierce faith and obstinate hope. Inspired by the achievements of the Moscow Arts Theatre, Dean had long talked of such a place for London, where the new poets and poetic dramatists could be heard. Brooke took up this theme vehemently, fired by examples of the new spirit in painting all around them jostling for their place with the established art of the eighteenth century. Everything seemed to be too damned established. If it weren't the eighteenth it was the nineteenth century. Classic art or bourgeois reaction. Even the Edwardian seemed no better. It was all too safe. Everything cut and dried. The standards set. God, how he hated convention, Rupert thought. Yet the world was good, too. Look at these wonderful people. After all, it was an exciting year to be alive - and a fateful one. An exciting, enthralling, engrossing evening, too. Each moment of it vivid, vital.

Rupert had his clear-eyed look of enchantment about him. To Dean he was freer in attitude and outlook than any of their contemporaries, a modern, born half a century ahead of his time.

Here was Brooke, in the small hours of the morning of Friday, 12 June 1914. Beginning to sketch the plot for a play he had carried in his mind half across the world to this stone staircase in Gray's Inn. Brooke epitomising what was the best in the traditional and the new. Diaghilev was setting the town in a whirl; Leon Bakst threw conventional colourists into a frenzy of dismay using blue with green for the first time. Rupert Brooke embodied it all, this fresh impetus in the arts. For he was of the theatre, painting and poetry. He was part of Flecker's 'Hassan' and the post-impressionist painters. He was young 1914.

And he was still living poetry. The final scene of this eventful night came when he solemnly danced to a Polynesian sway with a certain Jane, who had red hair and mouth, over the mown grass of Gray's Inn at dawn!

Nothing happened early on Friday! In the evening the Brownes, Marsh and Brooke met Lascelles Abercrombie for dinner at Simpsons. Rupert had not met him before, though familiar with his work and often quoting it. The man himself was small and shy, with spectacles and straight hair; he appeared wearing a queer little green hat which tipped up in front.

On Saturday Brooke and the Brownes had lunch with the Granville-Barkers but Rupert, for once outshone, crumbled his bread in a slightly jealous silence throughout the meal. So he was human after all. Perhaps the adulation this week had turned his head a little; perhaps not.

Later, he brightened up, as they picked up Gibson and Monro after an early evening snack and headed for the ballet again - this time queueing for seats in the gallery. Thronging the pit or gallery of the Garden and Drury Lane at this time were the leading young writers and painters, men later world famed. They all seemed part of the general new movement, and used to boast in fun that the most important audiences of the London season were seen in the gallery. Packed like 'ecstatic sardines' - Basil Dean's phrase! - they would rush out at the intervals to talk to friends or greet them across the uncomfortable, curved gallery.

So it was on this Saturday night. Then back inevitably to Eddie Marsh's and a mosaic of music, conversation, colour and dance. Brooke, Abercrombie, Monro and Gibson talked metaphysics at each other, and Browne, the entire night. Eventually Sunday dawned and the time came for bed.

Next day Ellen and Maurice visited the Gilbert Murrays, whose hopes for Rupert's future were great, while Brooke himself was arranging to take Abercrombie, Gibson and Drinkwater to a quiet place in his mother's new car to discuss the August 'New Numbers'. However this projected meeting never occurred, as Mrs Brooke demanded the car for some 'nefarious political business' Rupert wrote. Meanwhile, that issue of 'New Numbers' went to press with some of Rupert's best poems: 'Tiare Tahiti', 'Retrospect', 'The Great Lover', 'Waikiki' and 'Hauntings'.

Maurice and Ellen postponed leaving London for the Continent for twenty-four hours to enable Brooke to join them in London on Thursday 18 June for a final evening together. With Rupert and Cathleen - and the stage the bond between them - they dined and talked far into another day. Just before they all parted, they stretched their arms across the table and clinked glasses to the future - and the future of drama. Rupert's glass to Ellen, Maurice's to Cathleen.

Invitations showered on Brooke, one to a garden party which the prime minister held in July. He was asked to it through the usual channels of Eddie Marsh. Cathleen and Denis Browne were also invited. Brooke was determined to enter it in his extra-large South Seas hat, but his courage dwindled as he espied the array of top hats, formal dress, and splash of navy and khaki uniforms. Just in time it dawned on him that it was all very well being unconventional among his own kind but he could not merge into the crusty society gathering as he was - so he did not go.

'I'll wait for you round at Charing Cross Station', Rupert called to them as he loped off!

They left before the end of the party and strolled round to the station to discover him, as arranged, hunched moodily on a seat there nibbling at strawberries, still truculently wearing his hat!

July continued the merry-go-round of plays, debates, midnight suppers; Rupert was trying to make up for time lost abroad by fitting in as many events as each day allowed. On 5 July, for instance, he wrote one of his many typical notes to Hugh Dalton, whom he had not seen since returning from the South Seas:

Dear Hugh,
I find I can't get back in time for Tuesday night. I'm
sorry. I am free as the wind on Thursday night. Are you?
You can shelve your wife. Nothing shall occupy me on
Thursday night till I hear from you. Write immediately to
Rugby. All other times I am dining with E. Gosse, or H.
James, or S. Olivier, and others of my contemporaries.
How horrible it is to be a bachelor.

The meeting was sealed and Rupert picked up Dalton at his chambers in the Temple. They dined alone together and Brooke recounted all his adventures. The two men - still young - faced each other and smiled as they remembered the years before Brooke's voyagings. Those times when they were young in years. Now they were almost twenty-seven. But their young-in-heart outlook on life would never desert them, never change.

Brooke was the same Rupert that Dalton had known at King's, though more assured now. Yet despite his assurance their old eternal questions stayed unsolved. Perhaps because of this searching they would never lose their zest, however long or short their span. 'He made poetry of his questionings, and spared neither himself, nor love, nor the beloved.' So said someone of Rupert Brooke. And here he was, in July 1914, still a ferment of feeling, with all the impulses of man pounding in him.

During July he returned to Cambridge for a day or two and dined with Arthur Benson, who noticed a maturer person since the travels.

Brooke had actually asked himself to dinner, much to Benson's pleasure, and he talked freely of his three months with a native chief at Tahiti and many other things. Benson sounded him out about his willingness to do some teaching at Cambridge and Brooke responded readily, though admitting that he had no intention of making teaching his life. Brooke did not talk about himself to Benson, except in reply to direct questions. When he discussed the South Seas, it was more with the place than the person of Brooke. But Rupert joined most of the talk

with relish, even if he did not reveal any startling
sentiments. In America, he told Benson, he had found
himself merely a receptive organism, although he had
managed to grind out a few ramshackle articles.

The evening together passed easily, amicably and
Rupert idled through the twilit streets, seeing again with a
pang the silhouettes of the colleges and churches, exactly
as they had always been. And as they would remain. This
was as much at home as he could ever be. Still he looked
to Grantchester as a haven and gave it as his permanent
address always. The Old Vicarage. Perhaps he felt he
would be remembered best by it.

A lunch meeting, this time with John Drinkwater, in
Soho at a colourful little restaurant near Golden Square,
just far enough away from the bustle of Regent Street.
Elsewhere, another bustle seemed to be growing louder;
Europe looked threatening. Brooke talked to Drinkwater
quite eagerly about the possibility of his helping Quiller-
Couch in English at Cambridge next term. Through it all
Drinkwater detected a note of foreboding and disbelief. A
sense that Rupert knew even as he was saying this, that he
would not be teaching at the University, nor seeing
Grantchester. It was a tone which later crystallised into
the calm acceptance that touched all his deeds after
August.

By the end of July, he regarded war as inevitable and
went to stay with his mother from 31 July till 3 August.
At first, he was deeply anxious that it should be avoided if
possible and then gradually convinced that the country had
no alternative but to do its duty.

On 2 August he wrote to Eddie Marsh saying that he
would be going to stay with the Cornfords in Norfolk for
a week or so. At that stage, he had the idea of becoming a
war correspondent or agricultural worker in France if he
could not fight. He asked Marsh to let him know of any
job possible, but at the Admiralty Eddie had his hands very
full during the first days of August. Rupert ended by
observing that he would be twenty-seven the next day; he
had enjoyed July very much, though it was now only a
lovely vision.

'Do you have a Brussels-before-Waterloo feeling,' he
ended, 'that we'll all - or some - meet with other eyes in

1915?...'

He came down to London on his birthday and was in a music-hall watching faded meaningless acts when a screen was suddenly thrust on stage. A flickering film projector announced to the audience: WAR DECLARED WITH AUSTRIA. Brooke walked out into the streets. Stunned crowds were gathering around Trafalgar Square. Special midnight editions of the newspapers were already arriving and as he watched the people about him he was close to tears.

Next day, he made various futile efforts to get into something and then decided to accept the invitation to visit the Cornfords in Norfolk after all. Here he had time to think what to do. Mrs Brooke wrote that 'he hated the idea of fighting, his love of humanity was so great and his desire to benefit it so deep.' Amid the calm, flat East Anglian landscape, his mind cleared. He thought of days in Germany - now the enemy - and an April morning on the lake south of Berlin. And a Munich night with students who had sung, smoked and drank from 8 till 1. These things he would see no more. Nor would the Russian Ballet return. He thought of the words 'England' and 'Germany'. 'England' seemed to flash like a line of foam. Green, uneven little fields and small ancient hedges rushed before him, wild flowers, elms and beeches, gentleness ... At one moment he was in an Atlantic liner, sick for home, making Plymouth at nightfall. And then at last he muttered to himself: 'Well, if Armageddon's on, I suppose one should be there.' He didn't know whether he was glad or sad. It was a new feeling.

On 10 August he returned home to tell his mother that he must fight. A week after war had been declared he came back to London. The decision was deep, but once made, never doubted.

CHAPTER

13

In the stuffy summer heat from 11-24 August, Brooke tore over all parts of London trying to get into something useful and for a day or two even did drill in the faint hope of joining a corps as a private. After what seemed an interminable time he was offered a commission by Winston Churchill in the newly-formed Royal Naval Division. He and Denis Browne both joined the Anson Battalion in late September.

Some groups of the Royal Naval Volunteer Reserve were not needed afloat with the Fleet, so camps had been formed at Deal during August for shore service. These were the nucleus of what was known as the Royal Naval Division. The two brigades had their camps at Walmer and Betteshanger Park respectively, the latter lent by Lord Northbourne. It was into the Anson Battalion of the Second Naval Brigade that Rupert and Denis were commissioned. Eddie Marsh saw them off at Charing Cross Station early one Saturday morning for Betteshanger, looking very smart in their brand new uniforms. Less than two months before, at this same station, Rupert had been munching his strawberries disconsolately while the premier's garden party went its conventional course!

Betteshanger Park looked beautiful in the turning foliage of early autumn and far from the nightmare of war which was nearer than they imagined. Four battalions - Hood, Howe, Nelson and Anson - comprised the Second Brigade and Brooke's battalion was under the distinguished command of Colonel Cornwallis-West.

During the remaining days of September they carried out sham fights and night attacks, together with musketry training over at Chatham. His letters home to Mrs Brooke were full of the life which was so strange and new. Some of it he liked very much, the companionship and foolishness and fun; other parts irked him, though he managed to laugh these off. Taking it altogether, he was remarkably happy and began to feel that by compulsion, a purpose had entered his life. He rested content to let it lead him where it would. It was all out of his hands now.

Part of this abbreviated course, occupying only a week or two, was route marching. Rupert led his platoon along the Kentish country lanes singing such ditties as 'Hello, Hello, who's your lady friend?' and 'Sing a song of Bonnie Scotland' and the inevitable 'Tipperary'. He looked as if he were loving every minute of it and while they were marching at ease, he gazed around at the rugged hills encircling Betteshanger, as if inscribing them on his memory. Here was his England seen from a new angle and at a strange time. Different dimensions now.

Sunday, 5 October 5 a.m. Over the before-dawn air, a bugle blew and the voice of the brigade major shouted: 'Officers, get up immediately. We are leaving for France today.' Breakfast was at 7 a.m. The Second Brigade started to march to Dover about two hours later. Rupert was in front of his platoon, their packs on their backs, as they crunched the weary miles down to Dover pier. More songs passed the journey, and Brooke joined in them all: 'There's a man selling beer over there'; 'Wash me in the water'; 'One man went to mow', which occupied more than a mile and many more. They paused at midday for a snack and then plodded on right through the afternoon till the defiant lines of Dover Castle heaved on to the skyline and they dropped downhill to the town and quay. When the officers finally got all the men and baggage on board their ship they found no one had prepared an evening meal for the commissioned men. So a sortie into the town was made which produced roast beef washed down with lemonade and cider; and then all was ready for sailing.

About 9.30 p.m., just as the people of Dover were thinking of their beds, the ship eased away from the pier and nosed towards the Channel and France. Searchlights were trained on her, as Rupert lay down on an upper deck and dozed with a greatcoat for cover. The sea again, but no sound of gentle surf or palms beside the beach.

By 4 a.m. on Monday morning the ship had anchored off Dunkirk, where it lay hove-to for eight endless hours with the sea too rough to enter harbour. This must have been the worst possible treatment for all on board and they uttered a prayer of relief at noon when the ship finally managed to drag herself into Dunkirk.

Before the train took them towards Belgium, which they were supposed to be helping to save, Cornwallis-West addressed them and concluded with the words: 'Remember you are British.'

Dawn came as the train drew into Ghent with rain hammering hard on the carriage windows. Rupert remembered other train trips. Yet here he did not know his destination. It was 5.45 a.m., they were cold and hungry - but still somehow cheerful. A short stop and then on towards the war. A strange sensation, being conveyed right to the front by main-line train. Now it was 9 a.m. on the 6th and the first signs of war met the train. Away ahead, shrapnel was bursting around Antwerp and two captive balloons suspended in the sky directed German fire to the Belgian forces.

As the train steamed on Brooke saw, with a sense of tragedy, hundreds of Belgians building trenches against the enemy advance.

The Germans had been in a struggle with the Belgian army on 28 September and commenced a big bombardment of the outer line of defensive forts around Antwerp. The Belgian guns of mere 4- and 6-inch calibre were pitiful when opposed to 12-, 16- and 17-inch howitzers. It would clearly only be a matter of time. The Marine Brigade of the Royal Naval Division had been rushed into the defence on 3 October and the First and Second Brigades had been due on the 5th. Now it was the 6th and the situation grew hourly more desperate. Belgium was being ravaged - and savaged. The hope was to gain delaying time to enable the Belgian army to retire more or less intact to a line behind Ghent, where they could join the main British and French forces.

The Belgians welcomed the Royal Naval Division but it really arrived too late. Their train got to Antwerp about 10 p.m. and they were at once handed jugs of light beer which slopped over the top and ran down the outside. Girls rushed up to embrace the officers as they lined up to lead the troops. One flung herself on Rupert with flags and kisses and others handed apples and chocolates to the men.

Cries of 'Vivent les Anglais' sounded over the din of explosions only a few miles from the city. Brooke and Denis Browne led their little platoons through Antwerp and the outskirts till they were four miles from the station. After a meal, another five miles to Vieux-Dieu. Here Brooke saw hundreds of Belgian troops resting after days of ordeal. He wondered what would happen next, but did not mind now, for he felt the wound to Belgium as if it were his own. At Vieux-Dieu they halted and heard that they would be going up to the firing line soon. They heard, too, the bass boom of the guns, nearer now. No peace. The wounded came in all the time on stretchers and a horse was brought back from the front literally riddled with bullets.

The afternoon passed and they were quartered for a few hours in an old deserted chateau. The sailors bivouacked in the garden while the officers occupied the house itself. An ironic moment. From somewhere in its depths, a servant still there cooked them a meal of veal, bread and black coffee, which they ate at dusk by the light of a candle thrust in the neck of an empty wine bottle. The windows were plastered in brown paper for black-out and the distinguished group consumed the food like gourmets - but with their pocket-knives or fingers! As the candle flickered, its light fell on the faces of Cornwallis-West, Arthur Asquith, son of the prime minister, Denis Browne and Rupert. They drained their coffee from broken tumblers or milk jugs and all the time the guns boomed in the background, shaking the window-frames and the brown paper. At nine o'clock the candle burned low and its grease traced white streaks down the bottle; they rested quietly.

Five hours later, a Belgian officer stumbled into the darkened room and awoke the colonel. The time had come to move up to the front. Slightly dazed, they got up and dressed and went into the garden to the men. The fortress troops and the Second Belgian Division - all exhausted almost beyond endurance - and the three brigades of the R.N. Division were to hold the Germans at bay. The prospect seemed far-fetched. In fact, the whole operation savoured of the unreal as they made a romantic march through the night to Fort No.7. Every so often they passed

144

a sentry. Finally they reached their spot at dawn. Rupert could not remember the date but it did not matter. A year ago to the day, he had been heading south-west towards Honolulu, now he was here before Antwerp, facing thousands of Germans. And next year?

The trenches they had to occupy would not be much use, they understood. It would probably be bayonets. As the day of the 7th lightened all their eyes turned to the river Nethe. The forts fired away spasmodically. They saw trenches at the end of a turnip field. The day passed without direct action. A hospital had been rigged up in a bomb-proof dugout and stretchers were supplemented by blinds torn from a nearby villa. Then only a matter of hours after they had left it, shells smashed the chateau where they had sheltered during the night.

Now another night fell, pitch and cold, with a bitter wind blowing over the front. Suddenly an alarm. They started to fire into the inky blackness. Searchlights stabbed the night. Shells began to burst. 'Enemy approaching barbed wire' someone yelled, but it was only a reconnaissance from across the river. The fighting got no nearer.

A surprise attack killed seven Belgian gunners in the fort close to them but the Naval Division had hardly any casualties. The Marines had the worst of the fighting. Although it did not reach Rupert's brigade, there was no rest for them and by the 8th they were pretty exhausted, though still with some cheery spirits among them. Breakfast consisted of one biscuit, a piece of bread, a small slice of cheese and a mug of coffee.

As another day cleared, the shells got worse and they could see Antwerp deluged, a burning city. The Germans had got nearer in the night and intermittent shrapnel peppered down all along the front. Despite this desperate situation a lunch of steak was served at exactly teatime!

And as they ate, with their rifles and bayonets at the ready in case of need, the fate of the city had long since been settled. It all fitted in with the unreality of these Antwerp days.

Suddenly the drum-major said: 'We'll have to clear out, sir, we're almost cut off on all sides. They mean to throw their heavy guns on us tonight.'

He had prophesied correctly. Within an hour orders came from headquarters for them to evacuate quickly. Soon after their trenches were pulverised. They reached Scheldt. Nearby the Belgians had set fire to their own petroleum tanks at Hoboken to stop the Germans getting them. The fuel blazed brilliantly and its fumes proved too powerful for some of the sailors. Burning oil flooded one field and horses and cattle lay frizzled in a second.

Rupert looked back at the smoke in the sky - the scorching city of Antwerp - and at some of the hundred thousand refugees staggering with a few pitiful possessions. He swallowed hard. Then the fumes from the fuel blurred his eyes and he turned away.

'Now through,' he shouted, as the smoke and flame thinned for a second. 'Keep your heads and run through it.' They got through the fire, to a hundred yards of safety. Then they were exposed to a mile or more of enemy cross-fire. At last they crossed the river and the worst was passed.

Not all. The whole Division had to march against time to escape. They overtook thousands more refugees next day, who cast hopeless glances back at their doomed city. Then, at last, they got a train to Bruges. Denis Browne was suffering from sore feet by now, not really surprising. He was able to rest them a brief while at the Hotel Majestic in Ostend, before they sailed for England on Sunday, 11 October. Exactly a week had passed since the Brigades set out. Seven days inscribed on their hearts as a mixture of frustration, folly, most of all sheer tragedy at the fall of Belgium.

Fog stopped them outside Dover and it was not until Monday evening that they regained a footing on the good earth of Kent, surprised to see it again at all. They had not had their clothes off since the start and slept on the ground with no covering or else on the deck of the ship. Rupert was quiet that night as he lay thinking of those seven days.

After it was all over, Churchill wrote: 'The naval brigades bore themselves admirably under the artillery fire of the enemy. The Belgian people will never forget that the men of the Royal Navy and Royal Marines were with them in their darkest hour of misery.'

Towards the end of October Brooke wrote to Maurice Browne, now back in America, telling him of Antwerp and the Germans' guilt. It was clear that the smoke in the sky over the Belgian city was still smouldering in his brain and that he would not erase it. Rupert told him, too, of 'the other Nesbitt' being in the artillery and that he himself was still with Denis Browne and F. S. Kelly, a professional pianist who had won the Diamond Sculls before the war.

November passed with a number of irritating re-groupings among the various battalions, but by December Brooke and his officer friends were once more all together again in the Hood battalion. Now they found themselves no longer in Kent but at Blandford Camp on the Dorset Downs. It was a healthy, bracing place, but rather wild in winter and, of course, muddy. They wallowed from hut to hut and across the neighbouring countryside, but at least each officer had his own coke stove for comfort at the end of the day!

The camp was run on rigid naval lines, with watches kept and liberty men 'going ashore'. This last touch, however, was not altogether inappropriate by the time they had ploughed through liquid mud to civilisation. Each battalion had its own flagstaff and vied to have the best lines. In fact, the camp was quite a self-contained town of wooden huts, institute, Y.M.C.A. and even a cinema.

Brooke was glad to renew his knowledge of the Dorset Downs and, whenever he could, looked southward and remembered Lulworth and the past which already seemed several lives away. He had little time for contemplation, as the daily routine of drill, dress, boots and food had to be organised for his platoon.

Nevertheless, as he lay in his hut at night, he began sketching the form of a group of sonnets which he wanted to reflect the mood of the men he met and saw about him. The rain beat against the timber walls but he was unaware. Then, before he drowsed off in his sleeping-bag, he thought of the future and marriage. He wanted to have a child before anything happened to him. By now he had decided that he was not meant to marry. There it rested. 'It'll end in my muddling that' he wrote.

Cathleen Nesbitt was rehearsing J. M. Synge's 'Deidre of the Sorrows' for a short run at the Little Theatre. She and Rupert had resumed their love affair, conducted for a year by post and cable. They saw several ballets at Drury Lane before Cathleen was due to embark on a tour in a rather 'dreary drama'. By this time Rupert was at Blandford Camp and wrote to tell her that he could get leave on a particular Sunday. Where would she be on tour? The answer was Great Yarmouth. He was tickled about the name of the theatre where she was playing - The Aquarium!

Rupert made a 'hideous journey' from Blandford to reach the fishing port in the late afternoon. They had supper of fresh bloaters which they found ambrosial. Cathleen recalled that Rupert sat on the floor 'before the green-flamed driftwood fire and put his head in my lap and said, "Read me something beautiful."' She chose John Donne. Rupert said: 'Donne is always the best. He knows about love and death ...' Cathleen and Rupert scarcely saw each other again, though they exchanged love letters.

Christmas came. He was not due for leave till afterwards, so he spent the holiday keeping an eye on drunken sailors who insisted on dancing involved movements in their shoeless feet. The food was fair but Rupert decided it needed augmenting, so he sent a telegram to a friend begging for mince pies and cakes for sixty men! A strange Christmas, with the crisp air outside and the spark of warmth within from human hearts. Rupert relaxed for a day or two and pondered on this Dorset hillside. Where the huts stood had once been an Iberian fort against the Celts; a Celtic one against the Romans; Roman one versus Saxons. Here was England, its eternal earth beneath his boots. And here were its men, inarticulate but true. So, as 1914 ended, the five war sonnets were born.

Brooke was second watch for leave, so when the first half returned glumly to Blandford he was making arrangements for a dinner party in London. On New Year's Eve he proposed to Marsh that they should choose either the Carlton Grillroom or Cafe Royal. The vote went for the Carlton, where they were joined by Arthur Asquith and Violet, later Lady Bonham-Carter. This was Brooke's treat to them as he had just been awarded compensation by the Admiralty for the loss of some manuscripts on the Antwerp Expedition.

The night recaptured for a few hours the magic of the previous summer, but with a difference. England was slowly waking Rupert observed and it was rather a wonderful sight. The new spirit spread through all of them, and in fact their feelings were worlds away from the old days. Brooke told them of his menial duties as Sub-Lieutenant, R.N.V.R., and they toasted the year about to be born.

James Elroy Flecker died at Davos at the end of 1914 and Rupert wrote an obituary in The Times. 'His muse was stertorous with the lush slumbers of the East.'

When this was printed he was home at Rugby, spending the rest of his leave and finishing the five sonnets. He was also thinking more about religion. Too many people dismiss him as an absolute atheist but his beliefs were less clear-cut. Certainly he could not convince himself of any immortality, but belief takes many forms. He had a boundless love of humanity and its potentialities for good. He had little love of material things. These alone mean more than many people's observances. 'I think he groped, like most of us, in the regions of the spirit' said Lady Violet Bonham-Carter. And the splendour of the sonnets were the result.

By mid-January the sonnets were completed and as they were wanted for the current 'New Numbers' he posted them straight off to Gloucestershire. The proofs reached him as he stayed at Canford Manor near the camp, suffering from influenza. Within forty-eight hours he had written to Maurice Browne asking him to send copies of the sonnets enclosed to Harriet Monroe, editor of 'Poetry' in America.

'I wrote,' he said, 'under pressure of military labours, some honest but too crude stuff for the N.N. (New Numbers) and I want to get gold for it from the Yanks, too.'

They gave him some sick leave to recuperate from the 'flu, and he came up to London at the end of January, staying with Eddie Marsh first and then with the Asquiths at No. 10 Downing Street for a day or two.

Then followed a final interlude before the Gallipoli affair. As Rupert was allowed generous leave to recover completely, he decided to go down and see Wilfrid Gibson and the Abercrombies in Gloucester, before returning to Blandford. And at once he walked back in time to a village of poetry and peace.

Lascelles Abercrombie and his wife lived at The Gallows, Ryton, Dymock. Rupert saw its delicious black and white outline and stepped over the stone courtyard into a low-beamed room. Though the crimson ramblers were not in bloom, it still seemed as colourful and inviting as the first time he had been there just before the war. The earth was rich red loam, the hillocks covered with firs and birch. It was in the midst of the cider country and acres of apple orchards unfolded. In the spring, mile after mile of daffodils spilled over the ground.

Mrs Abercrombie met Brooke and for a minute her mind returned to his earlier visit and those other poets who had been there. John Drinkwater was very shy but very determined and read some of his poems to them straight away, with a fashionable parson's voice and eyes on the ceiling! He turned up with a sleeping bag with the intention of sleeping under the great elms at the bottom of the garden, but on the first night asked to be let indoors as a horse kept blowing at him through the hedge!

The sight of Rupert Brooke brought back to her just how wonderful those days had been. She had a permanent tent under the 'Seven Sisters', as the elms were called, and she saw again her iron pot on the fire, with a duck and green peas stewing in the spring air. Then in summers past, she lay on a stoop of hay and watched the stars wander through the elms, listening as Lascelles, Drinkwater and Wilfrid Gibson sat around and recited their latest poems. She thought that she had found the wherefore of life, with a mind at rest.

Eddie Marsh had also been a frequent visitor with his monocle fixed firmly in his aristocratic eye! He never minded the primitive house, although he was used to the comforts of London. Ivor Gurney was another poet Mrs Abercrombie remembered, seeing him first in khaki. Back at the front, an injury affected his mind; his subsequent verse was often spoilt by incoherence. The American, Robert Frost, received encouragement at The Gallows; W. H. Davies visited them just before the war; and D. H.

Lawrence, with the piercing blue eyes they met in Italy.

And now Rupert Brooke stood there again, in the pale February sunlight, talking to the two young Abercrombie boys, David and Michael, 4 and 2 years.

The Gallows was a three-sided house based on the courtyard, dating back about three hundred years. Inside its black and white walls and thatch roof, ran one long room which led into a hall, library and little room. Upstairs were two bedrooms and a dressing room, while to get to the other two bedrooms it was necessary to descend again. The bathroom was a curtained-off recess by a huge chimneystack in the courtyard outside. And the bath had to be filled with cold water from a long tube of red india-rubber stretched from a nearby pump! What did that matter when they could climb a high hill and see the patchwork panorama of the wonderful West country?

Mrs Abercrombie found Rupert as good-looking and glamorous as she had before, with an added beauty of expression and radiance of youth. She saw his tawny colouring and eager eyes, and found him still friendly and high-spirited. Although Antwerp had happened three months earlier he still seemed to reflect its mood and the recent 'flu. He was keen to throw himself into the thick of things and tried to tease Lascelles into joining him, but Abercrombie was not sufficiently fit.

Just before he left, they went outside, and Mrs Abercrombie stood beside him as he gazed at the garden and beyond. There in the summer, the huge sloping field, dropping down to the edge of the elms, had been ablaze with poppies scarlet in the sun - and Rupert had stood silently watching them. Now he looked at the field again and whispered: 'I shall remember that - always.'

CHAPTER
14

On 25 February, King George reviewed the whole Naval Division with Winston Churchill accompanying him as First Lord of the Admiralty. Blandford looked bright on this fine, late-winter day and the sun shone on swords and bayonets as they marched past the saluting base. Three cheers and the anthem ended the review. Now they knew they were bound for the Mediterranean. On the 27th, the last day in camp, they had friends and relations down to see them. Many for the last time, with Gallipoli their grave. Violet Asquith said farewell to Brooke and Denis Browne. The same day Rupert received, via Eddie Marsh, a pentagram charm to bring him back safely - given by a girl. He replied to Eddie saying: 'But what luck is, we'll all wait, and you'll see, perhaps.'

They left the camp at 7.15 the same evening, just after dark, wearing their new equipment with pith helmets and carrying a pack. They marched to the small station of Shillingstone, the entraining point, followed by mules carrying the heavier baggage. After an hour or two of the waiting, which became inseparable from service life, the train finally heaved out about 3.30 the next morning, Sunday, 28 February, for an unknown destination. They eased off their boots and slept through the rest of the night, to be jolted to consciousness in the 8 a.m. light of Avonmouth Docks, Bristol, where the Grantully Castle was waiting to sail in the early afternoon, convoyed by a couple of destroyers. The ship left the Bristol Channel behind by nightfall and reached the northern approaches to the Bay of Biscay next day, 1 March. She began to roll a lot as the waters of the Bay swelled, but the roughness passed, and by the following morning dolphins were sporting about near the vessel. A beautiful night heralded a calm day off Portugal and out of sight of land. In the evening, Denis Browne, F. S. Kelly, Henry Asquith and Brooke sang folk-songs on the sea air. Others in

152

'Winston's Wandering Wonders', as they were dubbed, included Sub-Lieutenant Arthur Asquith, son of the Premier, Sub-Lieutenant Campbell, son of Mrs Patrick Campbell and Lieutenant Bernard Freyburg. Freyburg and Sub-Lieutenant Tisdall both won the V.C. It was a brilliant officers' mess, full of wit and talent.

They were all excited at the prospect ahead. Mrs Brooke said that Rupert himself was exceedingly happy going out, commenting that if anyone could be said to be lucky in that way, they were.

Reflecting the fever of enthusiasm about this whole Constantinople expedition, Rupert wrote:

It's too wonderful for belief. I had not imagined fate could be so kind. Will Hero's Tower crumble under the 15-inch guns? Will the sea be polyphloisbic and wine-dark and unvintageable? Shall I loot mosaics from St Sophia, and Turkish Delight and carpets? Should we be a turning point in History? Oh God! I've never been quite so happy in my life, I think. Never quite so pervasively happy: like a stream flowing entirely to one end. I suddenly realise that the ambition of my life has been - since I was two - to go on military expedition against Constantinople.

As he sailed outward, the sonnets appeared in England, matching the mood, reflecting the feeling of everyone in the country so exactly that they would soon be remembered by thousands. Just the right amount of sentiment went into them. For war was an emotional time, it brought men face to face with life - and death.

In the evenings, when all became still, there was one officer usually pacing the deck alone. No-one thought of disturbing him, they knew by instinct that he wished to be alone. It was Rupert. He glowed in those quiet nights, drinking in their beauty after all the others had gone. He was only there through his love of England; the country he would never see again.

The ship reached the Straits of Gibraltar before dawn on 5 March and after Divisions, at 9.30 each morning, they had a chance to see the Rock. On the following day Brooke looked south this time, to the African coast and the white walls of Algiers nestling among the hills, with further off still, the snow-clad peaks of the mountains.

Patrick Shaw-Stewart came up to Brooke one afternoon and they chatted over books and people. Rupert told him how he was looking forward to reading Compton Mackenzie's next book. Mackenzie, who was to have his own memories of Gallipoli, later wrote that he had lived to hear Rupert Brooke sneered at as a romantic by the prematurely weaned young sucking pigs of the next generation.

They were north of Tunis on the 7th and put into Malta the next day, anchoring off Fish Quay. At mid-afternoon the junior officers went ashore in a Dhyear for supplies in the spring sunshine. The strong light cast colour over all Valletta and Brooke noticed especially the head-dresses of the women and the vividly green, shuttered houses. Then they dined at the Union Club and finished the day at a little waterfront cafe, being rowed back to the ship over the moonlit water.

By noon next day the island was receding as the Grantully Castle hurried eastward, past southern Greece to the blue-green Aegean studded with superb islands. They reached Lemnos on the 11th, and anchored in Mudros Bay, where a series of wonderful sunsets lit the hills of Samothrace with a rich golden glow.

Brooke would watch motionless from the deck of the transport as the dusk deepened, darkened. And it occurred to him that the time had come to consider arrangements in case of his death. He wrote to Eddie Marsh making him his literary executor and requesting one or two simple wishes. Then he felt easier and turned to a few fragments which he had been writing on the journey out. 'Golden phrases' he called them in fun. Much of this remained in his head only but what was recorded reveals that Brooke had reached at last a mastery of poetry. Like one of these phrases, his future was fated to be an 'ungathered blossom'.

A week later, they received orders to sail into Turkish waters. This looked like the real assault and an air of expectancy shivered through the ships moored in Mudros Bay. They sailed out on the morning tide and actually advanced some way beyond the entrance to the Dardanelles, but at that stage the orders were countermanded and they were told to turn round and return to Lemnos. The whole thing had been a feint, much to the disgust of all.

Back at Lemnos the rocky terrain made manoeuvres on land impracticable and the men could not be cooped up indefinitely aboard ship. So when a request came for forces in Egypt they were sent over to the flat expanses of that land on the 24th. Past the legendary isles of Patmos, Kos, Samos and Rhodes the transport plodded in good weather, reaching Port Said three days later.

After disembarking just outside the docks area, they pitched tents on the sand, where they encountered a virus which resulted in effects rather similar to dysentery. After a five-day sortie towards El Kantara and back, followed by a visit to Cairo with Asquith and Shaw-Stewart, Rupert returned to camp with a temperature and a slightly swollen lip.

The Commander-in-Chief, Sir Ian Hamilton, reviewed the Royal Naval Division next day, with their arms flashing in the sun. Brooke was ill in his tent, so Hamilton went to see him there, finding that despite his indisposition, Rupert still looked remarkably handsome. Hamilton did not want Brooke to take the risk of going to Gallipoli so he offered him a staff appointment at the base, one which would be useful but less dangerous. Rupert heard him in silence and thought about it, but after thanking Sir Ian, explained that having started this affair with his men he must see it through - at least the first fight. Hamilton did what he could, however, by saying that the place would be kept open for him at any time and had good reason to believe that Brooke would have accepted after the Dardanelles affair was over.

Meanwhile he arranged for Rupert to be moved into more comfortable quarters in the Casino Palace Hotel at Port Said, where the Naval Chaplain, Henry Foster, called to see him on 3 April. The attack of sunstroke - which it seemed to be - and the swollen lip left him a little dazed. Shaw-Stewart sat in the same room, also under the weather, while Foster chatted for some ten minutes to Brooke. Rupert pulled back the large mosquito net of white muslin hanging over his bed and his eyes flashed brightly as he assured Foster that he would soon be better.

The next day was Easter Sunday, 4 April, when far across Europe in St. Paul's Cathedral, the dean, Dr Inge, quoted 'The Soldier' - the last of the Sonnets - in his sermon.

The Grantully Castle was due out of Port Said on the 9th for a rumoured landing on the Gulf of Saros. Brooke and Shaw-Stewart both said they felt fit for the campaign but it proved to be another false alarm and the ship steamed back to the Greek Islands, to Scyros this time. A fancy dress party helped to pass the days en route and Rupert recovered enough to take part.

By the time they landed at Scyros on April 17 he was apparently himself again and started to explore this amazing island with its wild marbled mountains; glorious grape hyacinths; succulent langoustes; nightingales and goldfinches; and the memories of Achilles and Theseus where never a ship now calls...

Rupert mingled with the mountain shepherds, whose dress had hardly changed since the heydays of Greece, and breathed the scent of sage and thyme, balsam and storax. Here was eternal spring, he felt, distilled into a single day.

After a Divisional Field Day on Tuesday 20 April, spent travelling rough over the rugged ground in heavy heat, Rupert returned aboard and went to his cabin. Next morning he was clearly ill, his lip again swollen seriously.

The ship swung slightly to the tide in the roadstead of Trebouki. The bay looked like a lake in the mild April day, the light like a scarf about the peaceful hills.

Denis Browne received a cutting from 'The Times' reporting Dean Inge's sermon and his praise for the sonnet. He read the paper softly to Rupert, who managed a slight smile. Later on they decided to transfer him to the French hospital ship lying nearby, Duguay-Trouin. He was moved by stretcher to a cutter and brought across.

His face was bloodless but he gazed with large blue enquiring eyes. Arthur Asquith, tall and fair, came over with him to sit in the little white cabin of the round-house. Rupert was the only patient for this large staff, mobilised for possible casualties from the forthcoming Gallipoli campaign.

In the wireless room, messages began to arrive hourly. Sir Ian Hamilton was worried by the news which had been telegraphed to him and Winston Churchill was also in

156

touch. The only answer they could be given was that he grew weaker, worse. The surgeons struggled to neutralise the poison which seemed to have taken control. The tang of salt from the water, with balsam on the breeze, wafted into the cabin.

By the morning of 23 April Rupert had become unconscious and they gave up hope. Asquith sat with him throughout the day, until 4.46 p.m. a voice whispered:

'England has lost her greatest poet.'

So Rupert Brooke died on the same date as Shakespeare and Wordsworth. St. George's Day. The day of England.

> If I should die, think only this of me:
> That there's some corner of a foreign field
> That is for ever England. There shall be
> In that rich earth a richer dust concealed;

They placed his coffin in the poop and covered it with the flag. Sixteen palms lay beside it. The officers of the Duguay-Trouin laid on it a bunch of wild flowers, picked on Scyros and tied with the French colours. Arthur Asquith stood still, staring into the brief twilight.

They had already received sailing orders for the following morning, so the service could not be delayed, nor was there time to engrave a brass plate. Asquith called for a cauterising iron and by a circle of lamps - a wreath of watchlights - he seared the simple words on the oak plank:

RUPERT BROOKE

The little procession of boats glided over the water like gigs. The night was soft, bestarred, with a sheen of moon. The blended scents of the island drifted stronger and stronger as they neared the land. The boats steered for a little cove, as a pearl-white hue shimmered over the water.

The naval officers were waiting ashore, where they had put in earlier to find a worthy burial place. Beside these six were a dozen tall Australian soldiers, with broad-brimmed hats, as a guard of honour.

It was after nine when the funeral party started on its way up the gently sloping valley. Soon the course steepened and it was hard to tell whether there had ever been any paths, for no trace remained. The ground was mainly marble and the vegetation sparse; brushwood and little holly bushes, shadowy ghosts in the flickering lamplight. The lanterns lit only a few yards around and the petty officer bearers made slow headway. Sometimes they slipped or stumbled as the marble pebbles turned under their feet. Their boots trod down shrubs and a mingling of musk and pepper rose as incense.

The wan moonlight lingered and the flames from the torches trailed away in smoky tresses. No soul, no sound. The route became so unsure that men with lamps had to be posted every twenty yards to act as guides. It was nearly eleven when they at length reached the spot.

A perfect place, a mile up from the valley. Among an olive grove by a watercourse, dry then but torrential in winter. On either side, mountains flanked the ground and Mount Khokilas was at its head. Overhead drooped an olive tree. Around, mauve-flowering sage.

They buried him by the cloudy moonlight. Asquith deepened the grave and on the coffin were laid Rupert's helmet, belt and pistol - he had no sword. This could be his epitaph: he had no sword. A person of peace who went to war. They lined the grave with flowers and an olive wreath and the chaplain read the simple service. Three volleys rang out round the mountains; the bugles sounded the Last Post. Then there was silence. Forever.

On his grave they heaped blocks of white marble and at his head they planted a wooden cross. The six men who had dug the ground walked slowly down to the sea - Arthur Asquith, Patrick Shaw-Stewart, Denis Browne, Charles Lister, F. S. Kelly and Bernard Freyburg.

In 'The Times', three days later, Winston Churchill wrote:

Rupert Brooke is dead. A telegram from the Admiral at Lemnos tells us that his life has closed at the moment when it seemed to have reached its springtime. A voice had become audible, a note had been struck, more true, more thrilling, more able to do justice to the nobility of our youth in arms engaged in this present war than any other - more able to express their thoughts of self-surrender, and

158

with a power to carry comfort to those who watch them so intensely from afar. The voice has been swiftly stilled. Only the echoes and the memory remain; but they will linger. During the last few months of his life, months of preparation in gallant comradeship and open air, the poet-soldier told with all the simple force of his genius the sorrow of youth about to die, and the sure triumphant consolations of a sincere and valiant spirit. He expected to die; he was willing to die for the dear England whose beauty and majesty he knew; and he advanced towards the brink in perfect serenity, with absolute conviction of the rightness of his country's cause and a heart devoid of hate for fellow-men.

The thoughts to which he gave expression in the very few incomparable war sonnets which he has left behind will be shared by the many thousands of young men moving resolutely and blithely forward into this, the hardest, the cruellest, and the least-rewarding of all the wars that men have fought. They are a whole history and revelation of Rupert Brooke himself. Joyous, fearless, versatile, deeply instructed, with classic symmetry of mind and body, ruled by high undoubting purpose, he was all that one could wish England's noblest sons to be in days when no sacrifice but the most precious is acceptable, and the most precious is that which is most freely proffered.

One day soon afterwards, Maurice Browne opened an envelope addressed to him in an unknown hand. As he did so, the snapshot of Brooke, taken as the Philadelphia steamed into Plymouth Sound, dropped on to his desk. The accompanying letter from the woman said simply: 'If for a few days Youth walked among us, in its passing it left unnumbered years for memory of him who gave it so lavishly'.

So Rupert Brooke died. The legend lived and grew. A legend of a man and his work. Where does one end and the other start? How great was his poetry? Time has passed, time for the legend to fade and the worth of the work to be reviewed. Yet opinions still divide.

H. W. Garrod, formerly Professor of Poetry at Oxford, summed him up best of all:

It was when he got away from Cambridge that he began to be a great poet. For a great poet I do account him. He was also, beyond question, an interesting and rarely attractive young man, crowning vivid days with a death enviably romantic.

But there are people who do not like this; who dislike mixing the poet and his poetry. Garrod disagrees with them observing that, 'A man's poetry is, after all, only one part of his greatness'. Then he goes on:

He began to write really well in Munich. There for the first time you discover the real humour. There dies the charlatan. In the place of Swinburne now sits Stevenson. I wonder whether Stevenson had any effect on his visit to the South Seas? There he wrote 'Tiare Tahiti' and 'O haven without wave or tide', two poems I do not know how to praise enough. He has in his most characteristic poetry an ingenuity unbeaten outside Marvell. It came to him from the metaphysical poets to whom - and Donne especially - he became more and more bound. Some of his effects I cannot easily match in the last 300 years. He has a large Elizabethan utterance. Rupert Brooke has left us 25 poems of the first-rate. Yet the man himself is a fine addition to these.

The actual number of poems does not matter, nor which are thought best. That must always remain a question of personal preference. The vital thing is that although he died so young, Rupert Brooke has left us a living force of poetry, imperishable, inspired.